FLUSH THE B.S.
Reframe Your Life and Transform Your Truth

BY

DR. STEVEN CRANE

All rights reserved under International and Pan-American copyright Conventions. Published/Manufactured in the United States of America.

Cover design by Dr. Steven Crane
Edited by Natalie June Reilly

No part of this publication may be reproduced or transmitted in any form or by any means, electronic or mechanical, including photocopy, recording or any information storage and retrieval system, without express written permission of author.

Copyright © 2023 Dr. Steven Crane
All rights reserved.
ISBN: 979-8-218-21250-6

*To my psychologist, Dr. Elizabeth Lynne Barrett,
the person who saved my life ...*

This book is dedicated to you. It is a testament to your unwavering commitment, compassion, and support. You have been a guiding light in my life, showing me the way forward when I was lost in the darkness. You have been a sounding board when I needed someone to listen and a beacon of hope when I felt hopeless.

You have a gift, Elizabeth, a gift for healing and a gift for helping others. Your gentle touch, your understanding smile, and your warm embrace have helped to heal my wounds and ease my pain. Your expertise in psychology has been invaluable to me, but it is your kind and caring heart that has been truly transformative.

You have a unique ability to connect with others on a deep and meaningful level. You understand the complexities of the human mind, and you know how to help people navigate their inner turmoil. You have been my rock, my confidante, and my champion. I cannot thank you enough for all that you have done for me.

Through your guidance, I have learned to be kind to myself, to let go of the past, and to embrace the future. You have taught me to trust my instincts, to follow my heart, and to live my life with purpose and meaning. I have grown so much as a person under your tutelage, and I am eternally grateful for your influence in my life.

This book is a tribute to your life's work, a reflection of all the people you have helped, and all the lives you have touched. You have inspired me to write about the transformative power of coaching, and I hope that this book will inspire others to seek out the help they need to live their best lives.

In many ways, this book is a celebration of you and all that you represent. You are a shining example of what it means to be a psychologist, and I cannot imagine a better role model for me or for anyone else who is struggling. Your dedication and your passion for helping others is truly inspiring, and I am honored to dedicate this book to you.

Thank you, Elizabeth, for everything. You have made a lasting impact on my life, and I will never forget your kindness and your wisdom. I hope this book will serve as a reminder of the power of love, compassion, and healing.

With gratitude and admiration,
Dr. Steven Crane

Table of Contents

Prologue: The Journey Begins
    Finding Your Way Back to the Person You Were Meant to Be

Chapter 1: The World *is* Out to Get You
    Brainwashing & Limiting Beliefs the World Places on You

Chapter 2: Life Can Really Suck
    Do the "Right" Thing & Shit Still Happens

Chapter 3: You are in Control
    You are in Control, Even When Life Kicks You in the Teeth

Chapter 4: Embrace the Suck
    Be Quick to Realize the World is TRULY What You Make It

Chapter 5: Meet the G.A.I.L.s
    An Introduction to What is Holding You Back

Chapter 6: Rewrite the Code
    Reprogram Your Brain for Success

Chapter 7: Everything is an Opportunity
    The Fun Begins When Life Presents its Teachers & Students

Chapter 8: Show Me Your Books, Friends, & Calendar
    How & With Whom are You Spending Your Time

Chapter 9: Outwork, Out Strategize, Out Improve, & Outlast
    Sacrifice for the Dream, Lest the Dream Be its Own Sacrifice

Chapter 10: The Dichotomy of Success
    Learn to Fail Well & Get to Know Your Turmoil

Epilogue: The Next Journey

PROLOGUE
The Journey Begins

"Life is a never-ending journey of reaching out of our comfort zone. We can always reach new levels."
–Matthew Donnelly

It was a cold and dark night, the kind of darkness that made me question everything I thought I knew. I found myself sitting in my car, broken down and in tears, wishing for the pain to stop and the nightmare to end. I had hit rock bottom. I was a disabled, homeless Marine Corps veteran, a young man who had served his country with pride—reduced to nothing. I had no hope, no dreams, and no will to live. I felt ashamed, defeated, and alone. It was the most terrible night of my life ... as a husband, a son, a Marine, and a man. The road that led to this darkness was a long and difficult one, and it began on the heels of my military service. Like all military personnel nearing the end of enlistment, I had a handful of options:

1. I could say "peace out!" and graduate to civilian life.
2. I could reenlist, sign up for another two to five years.
3. I could move onto an entirely new career.

For me, the goal was to leverage the Marine Corps and the experience it provided to chase after a career in federal law enforcement. I was excited about moving from the legal/administrative field into criminal investigations. To make this happen, there were several tasks I needed to accomplish. For starters, I needed to obtain a bachelor's degree in criminal justice, get professional recommendations, retake a military entrance exam, get a medical exam, etc. As determined as I was, I was able to check off everything on the list, up to the medical exam. This is where I got jammed up, and my journey began.

"Journey" is just a nice way of saying that the road got hard.

It was during my medical examination that "stuff" started showing up—medical issues, psychological issues, and everything in between. As a result, I was disqualified from moving forward into my dream career. In just a few short weeks, my entire life flipped upside down, and I was left picking up the pieces. The double whammy hit when I was informed that I was being referred to the Medical Evaluation Board. Apparently, the injuries I sustained while serving my country were so severe, I was declared "unfit for duty" and entitled to a medical retirement. Although I felt a certain level of relief, it was short lived.

A typical medical retirement consists of two six-month stints, wherein the first six months you live at the hospital. Basically, you go to treatment and make an attempt at healing yourself. If at the end of the six months doctors determine that you are infinitely "broken" and "unfit for duty," they begin the six-month process of helping you retire with benefits.

For me, the trouble began at my six-month mark. Everyone in

my chain of command agreed that I should retire (with benefits), except for one GS-14. This one individual at the top of the proverbial food chain had the power to impact my entire life with one swipe of the pen. That action resulted in my being given a 72-hour notice to vacate the base and exit the military **with no retirement**.

Nothing.

With that unexpected and undue thrust into civilian life, my Marine Corps career was over. I was ruined. My education became worthless. My body was broken. My dreams were crushed, and I became a failure in every sense of the word. As a result, I fell into a deep, dark place ... darker than anything I had ever known. And what's worse, I had no one to turn to for help.

I struggled to adjust to civilian life. I was haunted by the ghosts of every aspiration and dream I ever had, as each slipped through my grasp. I felt disconnected from my family and friends. I struggled to find work and was unable to pay my bills. Before I knew it, I was forced from my apartment, and I found myself scraping and clawing my way back to civilization. Yet, even in the depths of my despair, I refused to give up. I refused to let my circumstances define me. I was no longer in the military, but I was still a husband, a son, and a man, and I was determined to reclaim my life. I knew it would take strength, courage, and determination to overcome the obstacles, but I was ready to do whatever it took.

Before long, I was able to find work. I saved enough money to get my feet under me. I attended therapy and worked through my trauma. I reconnected with my family and friends, and I rebuilt my life from the ground up. It was a long and arduous journey, but with each step I took, I grew stronger.

Now, as I stand steadfast and committed, looking back at the path I traveled, I am filled with a sense of pride and accomplishment. I overcame the humiliation of being a disabled, homeless veteran, and I have risen above all the odds to become the success that I am today. But most of all, I am confident in my capacity for resilience, that innate power inside of us all to push through, even when it hurts, and everything seems impossible.

This book is my story. It is a chronicle of hope, perseverance, and the power of the human spirit. It is for anyone who has ever felt lost, alone, or defeated. It is for anyone who is struggling to overcome life's obstacles. Believe me when I say, life kicked me in the teeth while writing this book. For starters, I was hospitalized. I lost loved ones. I missed deadlines. I faced almost complete bankruptcy of one of my companies. My computer stopped working, and I lost countless files. Oh, and I caught COVID.

To be quite frank, I was STRESSED!

On the bright side, some really incredible things happened! My veteran company delivered over $1.5 billion in benefits to the veteran community. I was recognized (back-to-back) as the MVP of the financial firm I am with. My professional networking company crossed over 50 members in less than one year's time. I realized my long-time dream of investing in an executive health and wellness coach. I traveled (all expenses paid) to Cabo San Lucas, Mexico with my best friends. My wife and I built our first home, and the list goes on.

What is important to remember is that both the good and the bad are a part of the human experience—the hero's journey. And let's not forget about the ugly. It is **all** leading up to a courageous return home.

The purpose of me sharing my story with you is twofold: Firstly, a part of me hopes my story inspires those of you who might be going through a rough time in your life. I hope it provides guidance as to how to overcome life's obstacles. As with many motivational books, the author hopes to leave their reader better than how they found them. There is also the hope that their story will help people around the world become the best version of themselves. The same is true for me.

I want the best for you!

Secondly, there is a part of me that hopes my book lights a fire under your ass and smokes out the BS that is holding you back. I hope you read this book and say to yourself, "WOW! This dude is complaining about XYZ! He has no idea what hard is!" or "Hell, I have overcome so much more than he has or ever will. I will show him what perseverance and success looks like!"

And to all of that, I say, "GOOD! PROVE IT!"

I know there are people who have had it harder than me. I agree 100 percent! However, I also know there are many who have NEVER undergone any massive turmoil in their life, yet I am still lightyears ahead of them. The point I am trying to make is that regardless of where you are, what you have gone through, or what still lies ahead, life is brutal. So, unless you take charge of your own personal BS, your mental health, and your goals, life will continue to beat your ass.

"But, Steven, I had to overcome XYZ."

GOOD!

That means you have the capacity to handle much more than most. So, why are you not out there kicking ass?! Seriously. One of my favorite excuses is, "Steven, you have no idea how hard I have it in my life."

You are 100 percent right!

I have no idea how much you have gone through, but I do have an idea of how much more you will continue to go through with a woe-is-me attitude and rainy-day outlook on life.

Why?

Because at the end of the day, you don't have control of what happens to you, but you are in absolute control of your next thought, feeling, and action. Everything I have gone through and continue to go through is what makes my story so incredible. It is what makes *ALL* of our stories incredible. Without the lows, there can be no highs. And without failure, there can be no success. Every person reading this right now has a story—highs and lows, failures and success. Perhaps you are in the middle of the painful parts of your story, or perhaps you are at the highest level of success you have ever experienced. Maybe you are on the verge of enduring intense hardship.

Wherever you are, you have an incredible story to tell.

The question is, do you have the courage to write your own story? The pen is in your hand. It is in every decision you make and every turn you take. You are the author of your own life.

So, write it well!

However, if you are good without the film-worthy "happy ending," and you would rather just go with the flow and let your story write you—great! Then do nothing. But, if you are prepared to experience the true hero's journey, be bold and courageous. Like the late Joseph Campbell, American writer, you understand that every great story in history has been set into motion in the call to adventure, in crossing the threshold, in the trials and tribulations, in the death and rebirth, in the revelation, in the atonement, in finding your gifts and in returning home with life's elixir.

The journey is bigger than you, friend.

Without hardship, we would never know paradise. Without pain, we would never know love. And without obstacles, we would never fully know success. The human experience is all about learning to live through various seasons of life, just as we live through the seasons of spring, fall, winter, and summer. With each season brings fresh emotion, experience, and opportunity for us to LIVE! This is not to be confused with a "Pollyanna" sense of "love and peace" but a true appreciation for the emotions we experience as humans. Additionally, this is not to be clouded by the quintessential "always-find-the-good-in-every-situation" mentality. The key is simply in realizing the emotions you are feeling and asking, "How is this serving me today?"

If you accept your current emotional state, acknowledge how

it is impacting you, then you are left with something—a choice. You can either stay in that state of mind or change it. Without a basic understanding of where you are emotionally, how can you expect to change direction and move forward onto a new path?

Let us take inspiration from Joseph Campbell's Hero's Journey which, simply put, is a character's evolution. From start to finish, it is the process of embarking upon a great adventure, a call to action that puts said character face-to-face with extraordinary obstacles that, ultimately, lead a hero home, only a better person than before and having served the greater good along the way. It was Joseph Campbell, himself, who said, "You are the hero of your own story."

Therefore, you get to choose.

Campbell taught us that the Hero's Journey is not just for "classical heroes," but for all of us. He said, "It's a fundamental experience that everyone has to undergo." With that in mind, as we reflect on the Hero's Journey, we can see the parallels in our own lives. We, too, have faced challenges and obstacles, but it is the way in which we choose to overcome them that makes all the difference. It is the choice to keep moving forward, to keep believing in ourselves, and to own who we are and know that we are, indeed, the hero of our own story.

That is what ultimately transforms our truth.

Friend, no matter what comes your way, you have the strength and resilience to overcome it. Together, let us reframe our lives, transform our truth, and take on the world with renewed hope and confidence. The journey will eventually end one day, but with each and every step we take, we move closer to becoming who we were born to be.

Look, my life is far from sunshine and rainbows. However, every day I wake up and I CHOOSE my path. I CHOOSE my feelings, and I CHOOSE my response to the world around me.
Although my current reality might not be the best, I have the power to change that through the stories I tell myself and others. The words I speak influence the thoughts I have, which directly translates to the behaviors I choose and the impact I have. Proverbs 18:21 reads, "Death and life are in the power of the tongue, and those who love it will eat its fruits." That is to say, a good word brings delight, but a bad word brings destruction. This is not only in the things we say to each other, but more importantly, the things we say to ourselves.

The most influential person in your life is YOU!

YOU have the power to stay in bed or kick the covers off and go out into your community and make a difference. YOU have the power to change your path, your feelings, and your response to the world around you and embark upon a brand-new life. Above all, YOU have the power to change your own BS, taking control of a situation, throwing your world off its axis, and experiencing things you never thought possible!

Life is a continuous journey, filled with ups and downs, twists and turns, and unexpected detours and dead ends. Throughout your life, you will continue to face new challenges, learn new lessons, and grow as an individual. And when you reach the end of your life, I hope you can look back in awe at all that you accomplished. We are the sum of all that we have endured, and I hope you go out of this world resilient, knowing that you gave it your best. Your journey is not about the destination; it is everything in between. And it is not a Hollywood script or even a motivational book. It is the self-work you do here on Earth that transforms who you are to who you are destined to be.

Stick with me. We can do it together.

If you are reading this, and you are on your own "journey," I hope my story will serve as a source of inspiration and strength, courage and determination, hope and encouragement as you work to regain your footing. Remember, you are not alone! You are not defined by your circumstances, and you have the power to reclaim your life, just as I did.

I promise you this; if I can do it, so can you!

No matter how far you fall, there is always a way back. So, take a deep breath. Put one foot in front of the other and start your journey forward. The road may be long and difficult, but it is worth it. And with each step you take, you, too, will grow stronger. You will heal, and you will find your way back to the person you were always meant to be.

So, let's begin!

CHAPTER ONE
The World *is* Out to Get You

"When everything seems to be going against you, remember that the airplane takes off against the wind, not with it."
–Henry Ford, American industrialist

What a fantastic way to kick off a book, huh?! To tell you the truth: Everything in the world is conspiring against you. Think about it. As you were growing up, your friends and family fed you their own BS, including your teachers, coaches, and other grownups in your life.

And your parents were first in line!

By the way, when I say "BS," what I mean to say is "Belief Systems," a set of principles or tenets which form the basis of a religion, philosophy, or moral code. Get your head out of the gutter.

I know what you were thinking.

The moment we are born, we are subjected to a wide variety of belief systems, whether we like it or not. It is how we make sense of the world. You have probably been exposed to a few of the following beliefs:

"Rich people are bad."

"Money is the root of all evil."

"Waste not, want not."

"Those who are good will be rewarded and go to heaven."

"Taxes are a form of theft."

The list could go on—indefinitely!

But what is it that brings these things into reality? Do they even make sense? Who gets to make the rules?

Growing up, I was constantly brainwashed with the BS of others. Because I was young and naive, I always believed what I was told. My mother had health problems, and she was deaf. My father worked a lot, so I did not get to spend much time with him. My family was extremely religious and conservative, and I was brought up in that environment. I was repeatedly told that "providing universal healthcare to every American would be a terrible idea," and yet my family was crippled by medical debt.

In addition, I was told that "Democrats are evil" because they advocated for better working conditions and wages that are adequate for workers to survive on, yet I hardly saw my father because he had to work multiple jobs just to pay the bills.

I had a hard time wrapping my head around this belief system, but as a child growing up in that environment, I began to imitate my parents' behavior because they were the ones in authority. In school, we were constantly reminded how important good penmanship was because one day we would need to write a lot of professional letters, and yet here I am writing this book on a computer and sending most of my correspondence via email and text message.

We were also told that if we did well in school, we would have a better chance of getting into a good college and landing a good job, yet wages have been stagnant for decades. Many jobs have been automated, and college admissions look at so much more than just grades. Besides that, less than half of college graduates are working in their field of study.

Does any of this ring true for you?

If so, it is probably because we have ALL been fed the same B.S! Permit me to advance the discussion by briefly touching on the subject of predictive programming, a theory that claims government or groups of elites are using fictional books and movies as a mass mind control tool to make people more accepting of future planned events. Have you paid attention to the kinds of advertisements that air during sporting events, like football, baseball, and basketball?

These advertisements often consist of girls, booze, big trucks, chips, and television shows. Have you noticed the kinds of commercials that air during other sporting events, like golf, polo, and tennis? Typical examples include Rolex, life insurance, health and wellness consulting, and financial services. Doesn't that make you laugh or at least wonder?

It should.

The very media that we consume helps to keep middle-class and lower-class Americans in debt, programmed, and depressed. This is the media's intent—subliminal BS. Growing up, I was always fed nonsense, and it didn't matter where I turned. It's because the world is always trying to keep people down, comfortable with the status quo.

If a kid disobeys his parents, people immediately view him as defiant. If a student disobeys the teacher and asks questions in class, people often view her as disruptive. This type of free-thinking creates a negative stigma. I have personal experience with this and can attest to its validity.

When I was younger, I had a lot of fun reading and learning new things. I spent a lot of time staring up at the sky, imagining the possibilities of what might be. To some, this sort of behavior could be considered "weird," landing me in an awkward social situation. Consequently, I never had any friends because other kids my age were interested in "cool" things. I preferred hanging out with adults in order to gain knowledge and insight from their years of experience. You could say, I had a very difficult childhood, marked by isolation, bullying, and physical conflict.

Despite the fact that I have a high IQ, and I always received excellent grades in school, I developed an intense aversion to acquiring new knowledge. Since I equated learning to being unloved and unlikeable, I gave up on trying to better myself. If enjoying my life, doing what I loved and asking questions was going to bring me a world of conflict, death threats, and torment, then why would I bother?

This BS was a result of my environment.

This belief system did not serve me well. In fact, it became the root cause of severe depression and anxiety. The very idea of going to school filled me with dread because I knew I would either be harassed, beaten up, or far worse. It felt like everyone was out to get me, and I am sure I am not alone in this feeling. Many of you can probably relate to my experience and the idea that the world does, indeed, conspire against you.

Have you ever felt like everyone was working against you?

You feel as though no matter what you do, you just can't get a break, right? This is a widespread sentiment, but it is also a perilous one. When you allow yourself to believe that the world is out to get you, you begin to perceive danger and difficulty in every situation. As a result, you develop paranoia and anxiety, and your pessimistic outlook on life makes you less successful.

So, what causes this sensation in the first place?

Beginning at a very young age, we are all susceptible to the influence of those closest to us. Our parents, family members, friends, and environment contribute to the formation of our perspective as it relates to the wider world. These people, whether they realize it or not, implant limiting beliefs in our heads by telling us what we are capable of and what we are not capable of. Unknowingly, we internalize these beliefs.

We make them our own.

For instance, it is possible that your parents told you that you were not very good at math, which is why you did not put much effort into achieving success in that area of study. It is also possible that someone told you that you lacked athleticism, which is why you never joined team sports. These seemingly insignificant comments can have a profound influence on how you perceive yourself and the capabilities you lack or possess. And your families and friends are not the only people who have an impact on you.

There are many different factors that influence your beliefs and perceptions, including the media, society, and even the government. Think about it; you are constantly inundated with messages telling you what to think, how to act, and what products to purchase. When "Big Brother" is constantly telling you what to do and how to do it, it is not surprising that you might feel as though the world is conspiring against you, especially when you feel differently than the messages that you hear every day.

Yes, this reads like gloom and doom!

The truth is life is difficult, and even though the aforementioned influencers in your life may want what is best for you, the people who love you the most can often be the very source of your suffering. Those who are supposed to shield you from harm and boost your self-esteem are frequently the ones who cause the most mental and spiritual anguish. That is not to imply that these individuals do not love you.

It is quite the contrary.

They are simply passing down belief systems that were handed down to them, stuff that "protected" them from far worse suffering. It is because they love you that their BS has been passed down from generation to generation. Your family and friends are merely looking out for your best interest by relaying information they believe to be accurate. It is all in the hope that it will be of some assistance in how you live your life.

Despite their best intentions, the impact can be damaging. By feeding you their BS, your loved ones (and your environment) have implanted some of their nonsense into your brain, which you will have to carry around for the rest of your life.

So, what are you supposed to do?! Put up with it and accuse

your parents of causing all of your life problems? Should you blame society for rotting your mind? Do you lean on the government to help you recover from the trauma that has been passed down from generation to generation? My response is probably not what you are hoping to hear, and after I tell you this, you might even decide to stop reading this book, but my honest answer to these questions is a resounding NO WAY!

It is not necessary, nor is it effective to place blame in order to find a solution to this issue. To be empowered, you are first required to accept and take ownership of any limiting beliefs that hold you back. Accept these beliefs as a reality in your life, and then take ownership in resolving them. Empower yourself with the right tools (like this book!) to move past the BS in your life and set forth into a new world of possibilities!

CHAPTER TWO
Life Can Really Suck

*"All our words are but crumbs that fall
down from the feast of the mind."*
– Khalil Gibran, Lebanese-American writer, poet

I f the previous chapter did not give you a sufficient beating, hopefully this one will do the trick! The unfortunate truth about life is this: It stinks!

People are always going to try to bring you down. The government wants to control you. The media makes money from keeping you entertained with fear. Your place of employment needs you to shut up and do what you are told, and to tell you the truth, the majority of your friends and family would not be in your life if they were not getting something from you. Presumably, you are thinking to yourself, "Yeah, but ..."

Listen, I am going to double down in this chapter, reiterating the reality that the world is a dark and dreary place. If you see where I am going, then congrats! You are nearing an understanding of my objective.

Stay tuned for further updates on that front.

In life, there are always going to be highs and lows, but there will also be moments when you feel as though you just can't catch a break. You are attempting to pay the bills by working two jobs, but then your car gets a flat tire in the middle of your second shift. You decide to further your education in order to advance your professional prospects, but the economy takes an unfortunate turn for the worst. You plan a daily workout routine to get in shape, but suddenly you find yourself in the hospital and in need of emergency surgery.

It is ALWAYS one thing or another!

You are not the only individual dealing with these kinds of problems, as I can personally attest.

In a similar manner, you may have concluded that you need to increase the amount of money in your savings account so you can prepare for the worst-case scenario. However, just as soon as you deposit a little nest egg into your account, everything that could possibly go wrong does go wrong.

Why does this happen?

Why is it that some people seem to sail through life unscathed, while others are constantly being struck by the slings and arrows life throws at them? Again, my response to this inquiry is one that you might not be hoping for, but the fact of the matter is that everything that happens to you begins with you.

Yes, you!

As a child, I had a severe phobia of germs, so I took frequent showers. I constantly washed my hands, avoiding people whenever possible, and I kept a clean environment. Nevertheless, on a regular basis, I suffered from a wide variety of illnesses.

Now, there are going to be some who suggest the "medical reason" for my getting sick was that I was unable to build up an immune system since I was not exposed to a variety of germs. Given my travel and sports exposure, this was not necessarily the case, as I was usually around more children than most others my age. So, what exactly was the reason for my being sick all the time? Let me tell you.

I never stopped thinking about it!

I literally attracted illness into my life with my thoughts. I made such a conscious effort *not* to become ill, that becoming ill was all I could think about. As a result, I took extraordinary measures to protect myself. The problem is the idea of germs and sickness was so entrenched in my psyche that it was *the* only thing I focused on. Therefore, I attracted that energy into my life, and it literally made me sick.

Don't believe me?

Ask yourself this: What is it the one thing most difficult to do when you are trying to lose weight?

Curb your appetite!

What is the most difficult step to take when you are attempting to get out from under your financial obligations?

Pay off your debt!

When you are actively trying to avoid being involved in an accident, the most common outcome is that YOU ARE INVOLVED IN AN ACCIDENT! When your subconscious mind is focused on something, whether it is "good" or "bad," the universe will begin to deliver more of that which you are focused on.

The outcome of your everyday thoughts, activities, and behaviors is a byproduct. That is to say, you are choosing to move your life in that direction based on what you are thinking. That is why focusing on the outcome is never an effective method to setting a goal. The outcome is merely more of what you are thinking about.

Rather than concentrating on the avoidance of illness, I shifted my mindset. I repeatedly said to myself, "I make healthy decisions." As a result, I enjoy good health. This transformation in thinking is not only subtle but strong. It is not idle chatter but rather has origins in psychosomatic treatment. The mind is a tremendously powerful tool, yet the majority of us have been socialized to believe that we should not question anything. Instead, we take this BS at face value.

I say, "FLUSH THAT BS RIGHT NOW!"

The outside world is a dangerous and unsettling place, but you have complete command over your own life, the results of your actions, and your own ideas. If, and *only if*, you learn how to govern your own mind, freeing it from other people's BS, the reality that you want for your life will be yours, and success will soon follow.

The most effective approach in grasping this idea is to first acknowledge the premise that whatever YOU THINK is, in every respect, correct. For instance, I believe that ghosts exist in the world. There is nothing you can say or do that will convince me otherwise.

The exciting aspect is that regardless of what happens or anyone else says, I will keep thinking (and believing) that ghosts exist, and because I think it, the universe continually shows me that I am correct. I am attracting this belief into my life, which means that I am drawing it to me. You may not believe in ghosts, but you will continue to have physical or spiritual affirmations in your life that reinforce your beliefs.

You will be drawing them to you, just as I am.

In a similar vein, if you do not believe in ghosts, you will continue to attract affirmations that substantiate your belief. The beautiful thing is that neither one of us is wrong. The beliefs we have generate a distortion in the way we perceive the world. The universe we have made for ourselves is nothing more than a contrived story we or others have created. These tales leave their mark on every aspect of our lives, for better or for worse.

If you convince yourself that people are out to get you, then I promise you, people are going to be 100 percent out to get you. What you think, you bring about. Now, does that mean if people have a deep care and love for you that nothing bad will ever happen?

No, of course not.

However, it does suggest that it is better to believe the best in others. Nevertheless, the proportion of positive to negative experiences that you inadvertently draw into your life is entirely determined by your predominant thoughts, feelings, and deeds. Therefore, you cannot "wish" your way to happiness nor can you "fake it till you make it." Every thought, action, behavior, feeling, and belief must be connected to your authentic way of thinking.

The most difficult experience of my life as a man, a husband, and a son was when I became a homeless veteran. I lost everything I owned. It was all taken from me. It was during this struggle that people told me to "maintain a positive attitude" and "keep my head up." The advice was meant to inspire me, so that I would look up and see the opportunities that would get me out of my predicament. While these folks had the best of intentions, they left out the key idea that underlies positivity, which is that you actually have to BELIEVE the positive stuff you are telling yourself.

Again, I guarantee that even if you reassure yourself 100 times every single day in front of the mirror that you are confident, nothing will change. However, try saying the words just once, "I am confident!" Then look for ways to demonstrate confidence. It helps if, in that moment, you look back on experiences in your life when you screamed confidence.

Harness that feeling.

Embrace the emotions and allow that surge of self-assuredness to fill your headspace. Mark my words; your actions moving forward will reflect the actions of someone who possesses confidence.

What gives rise to this?

When you think of something—a sad event or the laughter of a child—you almost always experience a feeling as a result of your thinking. Think back to a time when you and your family went on vacation or traveled to a destination that was enjoyable. You likely experienced positive emotions, such as pleasure, calm, happiness, etc. It is possible that the memory even made you crack a grin at one point. What would happen if you were having a challenging conversation with someone, and you started smiling because you were thinking of a happy experience from the past? It is likely going to alter the outcome of that conversation.

What causes this to take place?

Your thoughts and ideas cause emotion, feelings inside of you are stirred, which creates a distinct behavior or action. In fueling thoughts with feelings, you create different results based on what you are physically experiencing, and in turn, you produce a whole new reality by simply changing how you think and feel. Now, the same idea can be approached from the opposite side of the table. Think of a person you despise and focus on the reasons why you feel this way. Mull those emotions over in your mind and body.

How does that make you feel?

Do you not see how your tone of voice, facial expression, and the negative turn that conversation would take if, rather than thinking about (and feeling the enjoyment of) your last family vacation, you were thinking about (and feeling the disdain for) this person instead?

Of course!

Within that shift in mindset lies the strength of your mental capacity. Your thoughts draw various people, places, things and events into your life, and you literally have the power to mold your reality just by utilizing your thoughts. Thus, creating diverse experiences—good and bad.

I believe life is pretty freaking amazing! This mindset is coming from a man who was once homeless, living in his car. At the time, I could have easily given a thousand excuses as to why life looked bleak. Instead, I will leave you with the BS that changed my life and a quote from the late Henry Ford, American industrialist and business magnate: "The man who thinks he can and the man who think he can't are both correct."

CHAPTER THREE
You Are in Control

"I cannot always control what goes on outside,
but I can always control what goes on inside."
– Wayne Dyer, American self-help author

Life is not easy. There is no escaping the truth. Every one of us has experienced terrifying moments, when it seemed as though everything was going to pieces, and there was nothing we could do to stop it. It is precisely in these moments that we keep in mind one very important fact.

We are always in control of our own life.

I was the epitome of failure. I felt I had nothing of value to offer the world. I failed to accomplish what I had set out to do. My whole purpose in joining the military was to get my bachelor's degree in criminal justice with the help of the GI Bill. From there, I planned to gain work experience in law enforcement with NCIS, moving forward with purpose into federal law enforcement.

I had a plan; it just did not pan out.

Instead, I was unexpectedly discharged and told my military career was wasted. The worst part of it all, I was broken as a result—mentally, physically, emotionally, and financially wrecked.

My heart was broken.

My dreams were crushed.

My body was destroyed.

In addition to failing myself, I failed as a husband to provide for my wife. I failed as a son to make my parents proud, and I failed as a man, allowing myself to be in such a position of helplessness. I also failed in the friendship department because none of my so-called "friends" answered the phone when I reached out to them.

It was Walter Winchell, the late, syndicated, American newspaper gossip columnist and radio news commentator who summed up best what I was experiencing, and that is: "A real friend is one who walks in when the rest of the world walks out."

Considering no one was picking up the phone, that hit home.

Despite life kicking me in the teeth and feeling alone, I still felt a sense of power. It was not your typical "empowered" feeling of success or strength. It was more of an epiphany, a gut reaction. I said to myself, "Wait a minute! If I allow others to make me homeless, then there is no way I can fix this. Obviously, that would mean **they** were in charge of my life."

Suddenly, it was clear. The only way I could fix the problem was to take ownership of my "failures." My actions (and my actions alone) are, ultimately, what got me into this predicament. If I were to point fingers at the military and say, **"They caused my failures,"** that would mean only the military could mend them. Whereas, if I flip it around and say, **"I caused this,"** it puts me back in the driver's seat, and I can always fix a mistake that I make.

I like that better.

While in the midst of suffering, it is not uncommon to experience a sense of helplessness. Sometimes, it is even feasible to believe that the universe is controlling your destiny and that you are a victim to circumstance. The fact of the matter is, however, that you *always* have a choice. Even when life deals a hard blow, and it seems as though there is no way out, *you* have the ability to choose how you think, feel, and behave in response to your circumstance. If you take accountability for any given situation, then you are at the helm of your own life.

Obviously, this is no simple task. It can be difficult and daunting to get past the discomfort of a bad situation, and it can be even harder to conceive of a world where things are better, and you are not always battling. The unfortunate truth is that suffering is an inevitable aspect of life. We are unable to get away from it, but we do have a choice in how we respond to it. For example, you can choose whether or not to let grief define you, or you can choose to acknowledge and feel grief. Face it head on, and then move forward from a position of strength. You have the option (and the ability) to shift your attention away from things that are beyond your control and focus on that which you do have influence over, like the mindset to be grateful for the hands that are holding this book.

You have complete control of your own mind and your own ideas. Although you may not be able to control the stuff that happens, you are in complete control of how you think and feel about it. For instance, instead of dwelling on what you don't have or what you have lost, you have the option to focus on what you do have. Allow those feelings of gratitude to resonate and bubble up to the surface. Not only does it positively affect your mindset, but it positively impacts your physical well-being.

So, look for the silver lining in every cloud.

When you are having dark thoughts, struggling with purpose is, perhaps, *the* biggest hurdle. Because let's face it; if you have no purpose, then why were you even born? I can tell you from personal experience; it was difficult to convince myself that I had a purpose in life. I was homeless, heavily medicated, and I had no specific skillset I could offer the world. So, instead of trying to make up a random purpose for my life (i.e., find my "why") I focused on the here and now. Every morning, I would wake up and ask myself, "Alright, Steven, now that you are homeless, what are you going to do today?"

Dying was not an option.

Making the day purposeful and living intentionally was my only option. Though I was dealing with a ton of emotions, trying to figure out my life, I did my best to make every moment meaningful and significant. If I was doing something, I was doing it intentionally. If I was talking to someone, I was intentional with my words. I realized if I focused on the details and moved with intent, my life would carry greater weight. Thereby, giving my journey purpose. As weird as it sounds, my purpose in life was to make my life purposeful. I realized that I had to put myself (i.e., my mental and emotional well-being) first.

Like me, you, too, retain control of the actions you take—for better or for worse. You are at the wheel! Although you may not be able to control what happens *to* you, how you react is in *your* hands. You have it in you to move forward, even if it seems like an insignificant step. When facing insurmountable odds, even small, positive steps forward can bring about great improvements in your life and energy.

You can start with something as simple as holding yourself accountable for how you emote. Your emotions have a lot to do with how you feel. Although you might not be able to control your actual emotions, you can control the way in which you communicate them. Find constructive ways to express yourself, and do not be afraid to seek help from people you care about and trust. Let me repeat that; ***do not be afraid to seek help from people* you care about and trust**.

It may require practice, as well as a lion's share of courage to face and embrace your challenges head on. However, the more you practice choosing more productive actions and reactions, the easier life becomes. When you begin to understand that you are in charge of your life, the more confident you will feel. Even though you may not always get it right, at least you are taking the BS by the horns and making decisions for yourself.

*Remember, this is **your** story!*

Do you want to play the victim or the hero? When given a choice, are you going to throw in the towel or fight for what you believe? Think of it as a video game. You are the main character, and everything you do impacts your character's story. You have the controller in your hands, and you get to toggle your thoughts, feelings, and actions.

How exciting is that?

You begin to see things as opportunities to advance to the next level or gain a skill point. In the beginning of the game, it might seem pretty boring because you are basically running around acquiring skills, networking, and collecting tools that can later help you defeat bosses (i.e., life's challenges). But that feeling of control is important because *that* is what distinguishes a hero from a victim.

In the end, it is up to you to decide how your life will turn out. You may not be able to control the path that you are on, but you have the proverbial controller in your hands, and you have the ability to determine where that path will take you. Will you shrink back in the suffering, or will you face the parts that hurt and let it serve as motivation to move ahead.

I will be the first to admit that preaching this stuff is much easier than acting on it. However, embracing the fact that life sucks is step one in the recovery process. Just like in an AA meeting, the first step to recovery is admitting you have a problem. It is vital that you understand that these problems you face in life are a part of life. You have it in you to develop the resiliency to counteract these problems.

For example, recovering alcoholics continuously deal with temptation, but because they have accepted the fact that alcohol is a part of everyday life, and they have taken (literal) steps to keeping clean, they have empowered themselves to press onward in a healthier manner. In order to grow, that sense of power is necessary to move into step two, which is "NOW WHAT?"

Now that you know and understand that life is going to continue to kick you in the teeth, are you just going to sit there and take it, or are you going to face up to it and move past it?

Imagine your hand is touching a red, hot burner on the stove. Are you going to stop and ask yourself, "Hey, is that burner hot?"

"Yes, it is very hot, and it hurts!"

Then will you ask, "Would you like to stop the pain?"

"Of course!"

"Awesome, then do something about it!"

Chances are you are going to move the hand (i.e., change the situation), turn off the stove (i.e., stop feeding yourself lies and negativity) or throw some cold water on it (i.e., get help from others). To sit there and let your hand burn is ludicrous. So, why continue this suffering in our real life? When something hurts, embrace the pain and then take steps to move on and heal.

CHAPTER FOUR
Embrace the Suck

"Fear is self-imposed. You create it; you destroy it, too.
Behind every fear is the person you want to be.
When fear is destroyed, it comes back as confidence."
– Greg Plitt, American fitness model & actor

Let me tell you something, friend. The world can seem like a dark and dangerous place, and life can be incredibly challenging. However, you have it in you to be the light the world so desperately needs. But in order to do that, you must first embrace the suck! Now, I am quite aware that this might seem counterintuitive. Some days, it just feels better to bury your head in the sand or drown your sorrows in a case of beer because you have been led to believe that the world is supposed to be full of sunshine and rainbows, and that you should be happy all the time. Embracing the suck is contrary to everything you have been taught. But here's the thing: When you accept the fact that the world can be a dark and dangerous place, you open yourself up to the idea of something better. In embracing the existence of the darkness, you acknowledge there is the possibility for light. Then, and only then, can you begin to recognize the prospects for development and transformation.

When I was working for a repo firm, I was the target of a shooting. I was doing surveillance. Part of my job required me to get up close and personal with a few individuals who I shall refer to as "characters." One day, I got a little too close for comfort with some of these "characters." It led to me being chased in a vehicle and shot at. It was then that I came to a hard realization.

Life could not possibly get worse.

I had reached rock bottom. I was homeless, working as a repo man for $8 an hour. In order to save money, I would go days without eating. And as bad as it got, life tossed its head back and snorted its evil, maniacal laugh and said, "You think that's bad? Hold my beer!"

Enter bleak and terrible.

When I was in the military, we had a saying. It went something like this: "You are alright as long as you are breathing and there are no bullets flying overhead." I never really appreciated that saying until I got out of the military. It wasn't until those crazy "characters" shot live rounds at me in a modern-day metropolis (far from any battlefield) that I fully understood this concept: *No matter how bad life can get, it can always get worse.* Getting shot at was an extremely strange feeling because it put much of my military training to good use. At the time, I thought my life pretty much sucked because I was working around the clock. I had no money, no goals, and no ambition. It was all I could do just to survive. Being down range of gunfire was God reminding me that things could only get better from there. It would behoove me to believe for better, lest I get stuck in a job I was getting shot at for a living. I was starting to see the silver lining. So, I began to enjoy the small victories, like not getting shot.

I can laugh about it now.

Yes. Life was looking pretty bleak, sick, and a bit perverted for me. However, suffering was optional. I was fortunate in many ways. For instance, my wife and I had a roof over our head, albeit our car. And I had a job that paid $8 an hour. On the surface, things weren't looking great. However, underneath it all, I had survived a shooting.

Things were looking up!

Think of it this way: If you were traveling through a dark tunnel, it would be impossible to ignore the fact that there was darkness all around you. However, understanding that you are in a tunnel, there is the hope for light. That is to say, it is necessary to recognize the existence of the darkness and admit that it is present, all the while knowing if you keep pressing forward, you will eventually find the light of day at the other end.

Just keep moving forward.

The same can be said about real life. The potential for personal growth and transformation begins when you first acknowledge the darkness that surrounds you.

Embrace the suck.

What separates you from the darkness, however, is that you have the ability to **be the light**, not just for yourself but for others. You can choose to be the positivity and hope in the world. That is not to say that it will be easy, but it beats the alternative.

There is an ancient saying that reads: "What you focus on expands." So, if you dwell on the bad stuff that happens in life and you surround yourself with negative people, the Universe will create more of the same everywhere you go. If, on the other hand, you surround yourself with light, positivity, and inspiring people and events, the Universe will send you more of those good things.

It's true!

The reality is this: You can create your own truth, and the Universe will follow suit. According to the principles of positive psychology, the thoughts and attitudes you hold have an immediate effect on your level of happiness. When you dwell on the negative, you stir up feelings of negativity. However, when you shift your attention to the positive, your mood improves and so does your health. It might even give your circumstances a financial boost.

For me, the "light" meant making money because it responded to the pressing problem—me living in my car and not having money for food. So, I started working nonstop. My first shift was from 7:00 a.m. to 3:00 p.m. My second shift immediately followed from 4:00 p.m. to 12:00 a.m. After finishing my second shift, I slept for four to six hours and started the process all over again. It was hard, but I was laser focused on the positive aspects of my life, which began to expand and encompass my existence.

It was fascinating and exciting!

The harder I worked and the more I focused on the good things, the better my life became. The first step was accepting life's challenges.

I accepted my lot in life.

After I came to terms with the fact that the world can be a dark place, I saw room for my own personal improvement and development. I began to seek ways in which to make a difference. Secondly, I kept a good attitude. Every day, I made a conscious choice to **be the light** in the shadows. I concentrated on the positive aspects of the world and looked for methods to make it even more enjoyable for myself and for others. Thirdly, I put my plan into motion. I did not just sit around and complain about how terrible the world was.

My plan was two-fold: 1.) Never allow "homelessness and helplessness" to happen again, and 2.) Make sure I do everything in my power to ensure others do not suffer the same fate. The best way to accomplish this with no money, no social capital, and no experience was to condense timeframes and do what no one else had done before. I was going to go to school full-time, work full-time, and run a company full-time, all while volunteering and taking additional classes at multiple universities and programs.

Sounds like a lot, huh?

Well, when you have nothing to lose and everything to gain, you give it all you've got. And when you realize that you just wasted four years of your life for nothing, you have to make up time quickly! So, that is exactly what I started doing—EVERYTHING ... ALL AT ONCE! I did not pass on any prospects. I looked at everything from an opportunity perspective vs. an obstacle or distraction because let's be real, what would I be distracted from?

Poverty?

My short-term goal was simple, to get my feet fully underneath me and self-sustain as quickly as possible. My long-term goal was to get to a point where I would be forced to say no to certain opportunities because the abundance and success was overflowing.

I acted from a position of abundance, not lack.

What can *you* do to take positive action?

> ⇒ Get involved as a volunteer.
>
> ⇒ Give money to a worthy cause.
>
> ⇒ Be nice to people.
>
> ⇒ Buy a stranger their morning coffee.
>
> ⇒ Hold the door open for the person behind you.
>
> ⇒ Every little bit makes a difference.

Finally, remember that **you are not alone**. We all go through difficult times, but if we come together and support each other, we can get through it and discover more productive and purposeful lives. Although this may sound super corny, everything I have shared with you is supported by the scientific research of Dr. Caroline Leaf and Jim Kwik.

Again, it is much easier said than done, but hopefully you are beginning to see how I pulled myself out of a dark hole consumed with suicidal thoughts and negative self-talk. Too often we find ourselves in these "dark holes" of depression, wishing everything would just stop.

The pain.

The suffering.

The noise.

The sadness.

The regret.

From there, we spiral into anxiety. We feel helpless. We know something has got to change, but we don't always know what to do or where to go next, which causes even more anxiety, sending us into a soul-crushing depression.

It is an ugly cycle.

Trust me; I have been there. I felt everything that you might be feeling, and I also felt nothing at all. All I could think was, "Damn, I wish one of those bullets had hit and killed me."

I am not saying that my transition was peachy, but I am saying that if I can do it, anyone can do it. Start by focusing on what brings light to your life. For me, it was making money, so I could eat and save up a nest egg to move up in the world. For you, it may be spending time with family because it brings you joy and fulfillment. Perhaps it is volunteering your time because you like to feel needed. Whatever provides that feeling of "light," extinguishing that feeling of doom and gloom, do more of that. I promise you; in due time, your purpose will reveal itself to you in technicolor.

CHAPTER FIVE
Meet the GAILs

"Sometimes you don't realize the weight of something you've been carrying until you feel the weight of its release."
– Author Unknown

The narratives we tell ourselves have the power to either set us free or ensnare us in a prison that we have constructed for ourselves. In this chapter, we will delve into the GAILs of coaching, which are the invisible saboteurs that trip us up and prevent us from reaching our maximum potential and living our truth. These invisible saboteurs are referred to as Gremlins, Assumptions, Interpretations, and Limiting Beliefs. They are characters in our life story, so it is important that we acknowledge them and their role in who we are.

Gremlins—The Persistent Self-Doubt:

Gremlins are those pesky, little voices of self-doubt that whisper in our ear, telling us that we are not good enough, not clever enough or not deserving of happiness. They are the inner critic, holding us back from the idea that we are worthy of such things as love and success.

Gremlins can take on a variety of guises, the most common of which is reasonable thought and legitimate worry, and they can be found everywhere. My own personal Gremlin lied to me. It said that I was not intelligent enough to be a success. Even though I have a high IQ, I have never felt particularly clever in comparison to other people. I was lied to, indoctrinated to believe that the only way to judge one's intelligence and achievement was in one's academic performance on standardized tests, such as the ACT and SAT.

The foundations of our present-day educational system were laid in the early 1900s, during the height of the industrialization period. The initial goal of education was to mold students into obedient workers who were conditioned to adhere to a nine-to-five work schedule without complaint or question. This is precisely what John D. Rockefeller had in mind when he said, "I don't want a nation of thinkers; I want a nation of workers."

As a consequence of being programmed with such nonsensical ideas, I was under the impression that the only way for me to demonstrate my true intelligence was to obtain more degrees and certifications than my peers. I thought I needed to be admitted into prestigious programs to demonstrate my worth. Hence, I have two bachelor's degrees, three master's degrees, two doctoral degrees, and over 120 professional licenses and certifications. I can confidently say, "My Gremlins lied to me."

I have since come to the realization that the honest value I place on myself as a person is what determines my worth, not a piece of paper, not my grades, and not even the works I have written. What matters most is the value I place on myself. I get to determine my worth. It is not always easy, but we must find a way to identify and silence these Gremlins. When you hear your inner critic whispering into your ear, hoping you will shrink away from that which you dream, confront it. *Ask the hard question: "Is this thought based on facts or fear?"*

Assumptions—Beliefs Held without Being Called into Question:

Assumptions are the *untested* beliefs that we hold about ourselves, other people, and the universe around us. They leave an imprint on our thoughts, which in turn, molds our expectations and muddies our personal perspective of the world around us.

Ask me how I know.

In 2020, I was questioned in a counseling session as to why I decided to acquire my vast education, including licenses, certifications, and academic awards. That basic question led me down a rabbit hole, and I am going to share my findings with you, just as I did with the coach who posed the question. When I was a child, I was the target of severe bullying. There were death threats made against me, and I was placed in protective detention. I was the school outcast. I never had any friends growing up because of my reclusive reputation. Students made fun of me and because of the things I talked about (i.e., work, business, philosophy, religion, and politics), I rapidly detested going to school. For a kid who loved learning new things, I began to resist education in the worst way.

It was awful.

At school, I desperately looked for childhood companions who would play with me, and when I found them, I naively treated them with the same level of trust I would a best friend. In turn, these so-called "companions" would exploit me in various ways—physically and emotionally. They were usually the same age or older than me. My mental growth was severely hindered between the ages of five and nine as a result of the abuse I endured at school and around certain people. This experience profoundly impacted my childhood, along with my worldview.

Growing up, I never received any type of sex education. Therefore, because of what happened to me sexually and at the hands of other boys, I naturally assumed I was gay. I naively thought if I was sexually aroused, that meant I was attracted to that person, regardless of the fact that it was abuse. I spent the majority of my formative years under the impression I was a homosexual. I was afraid to tell my God-fearing parents. I thought that if I told them what was going on, I would get into trouble because, according to the Christian worldview, this was a major no-no. My parents and the church they attended are adamant that homosexuality is a sin. Again, this BS made me think I violated the rules of Christianity. As a result, I concealed it, and the merciless teasing continued.

Unfortunately, because my father was constantly working to provide for our family, I did not spend a lot of time with him. His lack of presence in my life created a meaningful void of a strong, masculine energy, something I needed desperately in my formative years.

Like Gremlins, it can be difficult to understand and acknowledge these Assumptions. It has been my experience that you must first check yourself; take a step back and take a deep breath.

Rather than making decisions on what you *think* you know, confront your assumptions.

Ask questions, rather than just assume.

"Is this feeling I am having because of something I heard, saw, or was told?"

"Why would someone tell me this information? Do they have something to gain or are they imparting wisdom?"

"How is this belief or byproduct serving me today?"

"Am I the one making this decision or is my parent, friend, and/or leader influencing my decision?"

"What would be different if I looked at this from another angle or a third-person perspective?"

Interpretation: Meanings Derived from Stories We Create

The stories we tell ourselves help make sense of the world around us. Our life experience, our cultural background, and our own personal bias contribute to the formation of our BS. These tales we tell ourselves are essentially opinions we create about a situation, an event or an experience in our life. While at times these opinions can be constructive, they can also confuse and warp our perception. It is all in how we interpret the stuff that happens to us.

For example, because I was bullied and sexually assaulted in grade school, I was of the opinion that I had to prove that I was ***not*** a homosexual. Again, I was assuming this was how the world saw me, and because I did not have a strong masculine role model in my life, I interpreted that to mean something it was not. In my young, impressionable mind, I thought if I was to survive high school, I needed to find a girlfriend and keep a low profile. Because of the ridicule I received for not having a relationship, I prioritized a girlfriend over good grades.

Girlfriend > Good Grades

Had I looked for other ways to interpret the situation, it would have lessened the negative effects on my life, including my education. Rather than concentrating on how to change the way others perceived me, I could have focused on improving myself and my grades. As a result, perceptions would have likely improved in a more authentic way. That is to say, seek productive and positive ways to look at a situation, considering all possibilities.

Ask yourself, "What is another way to look at this?"

Limiting Beliefs: The Walls We Build

Limiting beliefs are self-imposed blocks that prevent you from realizing your full potential. Simply put, if you don't believe you can achieve a goal, you won't put forth the effort and energy to even attempt it.

If you think you can't, then you won't.

The more you practice this limiting belief system, the more ingrained it becomes in your way of thinking.

During my senior year, I was approached by a United States Marine Corps recruiter. He told me that the Marine Corps could help build my confidence, teach me what it means to be a man. I laughed at first because I was all of 5'3, 130 pounds. In my mind, I was not exactly the poster boy Marine. Nevertheless, I saw this as a great opportunity for me to "man up." It was my doorway into law enforcement, a place where I could be one of "the few and the proud" to safeguard people. In order to do so, I would have to get over my limiting belief that I did not "look like" a Marine. That brand of BS could have easily kept me from achieving a lifelong dream. I could not let that happen, so I decided to challenge the limiting beliefs that told me only big, strong, manly men could join the U.S. Marine Corps. I asked myself, "What does a Marine look like?"

After some reflection, I could clearly see that being a Marine had more to do with core values and inner strength than outer physical attributes. I reasoned that if I could prevail over *this* obstacle, then I would most definitely be a "man," something I questioned most of my young life.

So, I joined the U.S. Marine Corps as a way to reclaim my masculine energy and demonstrate I was strong enough to make my own decisions and still participate in activities and pastimes that brought me the most pleasure, such as reading books and learning new things. My life would look so different, had I allowed such limiting beliefs keep me from moving forward into my manhood. Life is a series of paradigm shifts. So, always raise questions and reason with yourself and your BS. Don't simply accept the beliefs that limit you.

Ask yourself, "Is this belief true?"

Taking on the GAILs in your life story is an adventure of self-discovery and development that lasts a lifetime. It requires you to step up and challenge the internal storylines you tell yourself and to question those lifelong beliefs you hold. As you are able to identify and remove these internal barriers, you can start to rewrite the narratives of your own life, thereby releasing yourself into the great, wide world of possibilities!

After graduating at the top of my class in the Marine Corps, I immediately enrolled in my bachelor's degree program and fell in love all over again with education and learning. I had finally proven to myself that it was okay to love learning. I realized if I was good at it, then I must have been created to do something with it. It only took three years of psychotherapy and introspection to grasp it.

I share this with you because having the courage to own my own narrative, bravely addressing and overcoming my GAILs, I am a better man. Look, we all have Gremlins whispering lies into our ear, keeping us from becoming our best. Based on life experience and what we were told as children, we all draw conclusions about our life and what the future holds. We all have limiting beliefs preventing us from limitless possibilities. What separates you from the herd is in identifying those GAILs (Gremlins, Assumptions, Interpretations, and Limiting Beliefs) preventing you from moving forward, pinpointing the origin of your BS.

Since being bullied in school, I have made it my mission to prove my bullies and my BS wrong. I am so much smarter and stronger than anyone believed, not to mention what I was led to believe. It is as simple and as uncomplicated as that. It is in that vein that I ask you, "What exactly are your GAILs, and when do you plan to face them head on?"

CHAPTER SIX
Rewrite the Code

"Whatever we plant in our subconscious mind and nourish with repetition and emotion will one day become a reality."
– Earl Nightingale, American radio speaker & author

Imagine your brain is a sophisticated computer system, capable of performing a mind-boggling array of duties and calculations. The brain, much like any computer, processes and stores information using a language called "code." This code is the language of your thinking. Your brain's blueprint, also known as its "programming," determines how you make sense of the world around you and how you respond to the challenges life throws at you. In this chapter, we will delve into the fascinating field of "positive psychology" and discuss the various ways in which you can retrain your brain to live a happier and more successful existence.

The Virus That Infects Our Code is Negative Self-Talk

A negative self-talk loop is analogous to a computer infection, in terms of its destructive potential. It infiltrates our thinking and taints the way in which we perceive the world, ourselves, and others. If your internal dialogue is self-defeating, you can be left with a feeling of inadequacy, depression, and an inability to take the necessary steps in accomplishing your goals. When this "virus" infects your brain, it can be challenging to liberate yourself from the shackles that hold you back.

I remember a time in my life when my mind was flooded with negative self-talk. It was a mind-numbing loop of negativity. On a daily basis, I carelessly verbalized it out loud. I would say things like, "How have others successfully transitioned into a good career and a great life?"

"I am such a failure for being in this situation!"

"I must be such a dumb-ass, a real loser!"

"Who wants to hire a 22-year-old, medically-retired sergeant who is homeless and can't even get his life together?"

My personal favorite was, "I will never be good enough to find a job because I have no real transferrable skills from the military."

These, and so many other self-deprecating thoughts, constantly floated around inside of my head, weighing on my heart and mind. It honestly made me feel like I was going insane. Maybe I was. I mean, who walks around hearing disapproving voices in their head all day long?

The Antidote to the Virus is a Healthy Dose of Positive Self-talk.

Practicing optimism and positive self-talk can act as a vaccine against the virus of pessimism. It is the proverbial "software update" to your mental operating system. Your brain requires this in order to protect itself from the debilitating effects of negative thinking. When you engage in constructive feedback that fuels your mind, you bolster your ability to deal with life's difficulties, not only that, but you motivate yourself in the process, enhancing your overall well-being.

Have you ever looked in the mirror and started talking to yourself? Well, that is exactly how I got started on this journey of positive self-talk and daily affirmations. One day, I could not deal with all the voices in my head telling me how worthless I was, so I started talking back. I wanted to drown out the no-good noise. Therefore, I said the words out loud, reminding myself that all that negative thinking was not true!

I literally argued with myself in private. I had deep and meaningful conversations with my inner demons, and I didn't back down. When negative thoughts told me, "You come from a broke family, and you will always be broke! Just be thankful you found a job," I would come back with, "That is total bull shit!"

I said the words out loud, unyieldingly.

Many pull themselves out of worse situations than mine, successfully breaking generational curses. I knew there was no reason I could not break the cycle. I repeatedly told myself, "After all the pain and struggle I have been through, I **AM** worthy of success and happiness!"

Over time, I realized that these conversations (that still persist to this day) are the reasons I was able to drown out the negativity in my "operating system" and reprogram it to spit out more positive and encouraging thoughts about myself and my life.

What you think about, you bring about.
No truer words.

The Field of Positive Psychology Can Help Rewire Your Brain

The process of reprogramming the code in your brain requires an active effort in recognizing destructive thought patterns and substituting them with positive thought patterns. Listed below are techniques that assist in rewiring your brain for a more optimistic outlook:

⇒ **Practice Mindfulness**: As you recognize negative self-talk, stop and plant your feet in the present moment. Replace those negative recordings in your brain with positive ones. For example, instead of saying to yourself, "I am not smart enough to accomplish this goal," turn it around by saying, "Not only am I smart enough, but I am a force to be reckoned with." Let those words sink in like a wrecking ball. Repeat them over and over again, if you have to. Any time a negative thought enters your brain, repeat this practice.

⇒ **Use Positive Affirmations**: Throughout the day, even when you are in the shower, assert confidence-building declarations. Say the words out loud, "I am strong," "I am worthy," and "I am capable." In time, these affirmations will become ingrained in your thought pattern, overriding the negative stuff impeding the path forward.

⇒ **Surround Yourself With Positive People**: By putting yourself in an encouraging environment, you are more open to participate in life-affirming activities that bring you joy and give your life purpose. Fuel your mind with books, articles, podcasts, music, and conversation that promote positive psychology. If it means parting ways with toxic people and places, then so be it.

⇒ **Develop an Attitude of Thankfulness**: Routinely reflect on and communicate your appreciation for the many blessings in your life. This practice will teach your brain to concentrate on the positive aspects of situations rather than getting caught up in the negative.

⇒ **Seek Professional Assistance:** If you find yourself struggling with profoundly ingrained negative thought patterns, you may find it helpful to work with a therapist or a counselor. The professionals are equipped to assist in determining the reasons behind negative self-talk and provide direction in retraining your thought patterns.

The process of reprogramming your brain is a lifelong adventure, but with intention and practice, you can change the dialogue you have with yourself, and it will transform your reality. Like many of you reading this book right now, my entire existence has been filled with terrible programming. I was told that "only wealthy people can accomplish elaborate goals" and that "the only way I would ever retire comfortably or achieve the ideal balance between my professional and personal life was if I got a decent education and a well-paying job." However, the piece of advice that has been the most detrimental to my life was that I should "pay attention to my teachers, and act in accordance with their counsel."

Now you may be screaming, "WHAT?!"

You see, I was under the impression that having excellent mentors would help me get to where I wanted to be (Where I am today!) and that surrounding myself with wise counsel was essential. To some extent, that is accurate, provided you "interpret" the information given to you in a critical way, so as to make the best decisions for your own life. Not every piece of information you get from a mentor is gospel, particularly in relation to your life and the decisions you make. Remember the GAILs (Gremlins, Assumptions, Interpretation, and Limited Belief)?

Did you see what I did just now?

Listening to your God-given intuition and allowing yourself the space to truly make your own decisions based on the conditions of your life, the things you value, and the beliefs you hold dear is equally as essential as having mentors and receiving sound advice. We position mentors in a category where they can do no wrong because, after all, look at their success.

They are where you want to be!

This is a mistake we make far too frequently. The problem arises when we disregard our gut instinct and give these teachers complete control over our lives. For instance, a wonderful teacher of mine once advised me that "in order to command an audience and acquire a following, one must first earn respect in their field of expertise."

On the surface, this piece of advice makes perfect sense. So, I inquired about the means in which I could achieve this at a young age. My teacher responded by enrolling me in classes and encouraging me to pursue a higher level of education.

Mind you, perception is nine-tenths of reality.

That is to say, just because my teacher was successful in taking this route, did not mean the same results would apply to me. Our circumstances would have had to be exactly the same, which they were not. Nor did we share the same gifts, to say nothing of our abilities, our calling, and our energy. To put it succinctly, my teacher and I had nothing in common. But that is the beautiful part about this whole situation. Once you realize you are 100 percent unlike anyone else, and no one has walked in your shoes long enough to know where it is you are going, you realize what your gifts are to this world. And no matter what ideas or advice your mentor(s) have for you, it is simply a suggestion, not a paved road to your purpose! You will have to cut that path for yourself, and once you realize this, you will find that you are already on your way.

It is up to you to figure out.

This is fantastic news! It means you are no longer constrained by what others feel you should do with your life, not your teachers, not your mentors, not your parents, not your significant other.

It is all on you!

You, and only you, have the power to craft a life that is in harmony with your narrative, the values you uphold, and the objectives you have set for yourself. The question that needs to be asked is this: "What is the next line of "code" you will write as a means to transform your life?"

CHAPTER SEVEN
Everything is an Opportunity

"Everything is either an opportunity to grow or an obstacle to keep you from growing. You get to choose."
– Wayne Dyer, American self-help author

Every occurrence, moment (big and small), and person you meet weaves together, forming the fabric of your life. You are intertwined with the rest of the world, and within that intricate design, there are a plethora of possibilities. Much like the strands of thread that make up a beautiful tapestry, there are opportunities concealed in clear view. These opportunities literally hide in plain sight, watching and waiting for you to connect, so each can fulfill its function.

Every individual you encounter throughout your life serves as both an educator and a pupil. Everyone has something to contribute, and everyone has something to take away from every experience. When you approach life with this frame of mind, you can clearly see the possibility for development and metamorphosis. Grasp this way of thinking, and you open yourself up to countless opportunities the world has to offer.

Look at it this way; you are both a teacher and a pupil in this gigantic, educational institution known as the globe. This "classroom" is brimming with information that is just waiting to be absorbed and voices that are just waiting to be heard. Your life is a continuous conversation with the Universe, and every experience provides an opportunity for personal development. Whether you are the teacher or the pupil in any given situation, you have the freedom to participate in life and make the most of your potential for learning and development.

Stay open to the idea of learning.

Here is something to consider; when life happens, there are two ways of looking at it. 1.) Life is happening TO YOU or 2.) Life is happening FOR YOU. The difference between the two is significant in that life is a matter of mindset and how you approach different circumstances. A victim mentality might take on the perception that life happens TO YOU. This gives the impression that you are helpless and at the mercy of exterior forces. This way of thinking can lead to feelings of helplessness, frustration, and hopelessness.

On the other hand, when you see life happening FOR YOU, there is room for personal development, even in the difficult times. If you believe life is presenting opportunity vs. obstacles, it allows for growth and advancement. This mindset encourages feelings of self-determination and gratitude, helping you to see opportunity at every turn.

Take a moment to reflect on a time in your life when you were confronted with something that, at first glance, seemed difficult or impossible to overcome. Did you see this life event as something happening TO YOU or FOR YOU? In what ways did your frame of mind contribute to the way in which you reacted to that event?

We can change our mentality and make room for the possibility of personal development and progress if we simply shift our perspective and make the conscious decision to see the world as a series of opportunities rather than as a collection of obstacles.

Every person you meet acts as a mirror, projecting back to you the life lessons you most need to acquire. When you are aware of this, you are better able to see these interactions as an opportunity for personal development. Approach your relationships with a positive attitude and an eagerness to glean insight that each has to offer.

Stay curious and open.

Cultivate more meaningful connections and liberate the latent potential for change within yourself. Move through the intricate pattern of life. Recognize and appreciate your dual responsibility as both a learner and an educator. Work on developing a growth mentality. Look at every circumstance as a potential learning opportunity, even if it hurts. If you do this, you will unearth hidden treasures that reside within you, as well as open passageways that lead to a fuller, more satisfying life. In effect, you will develop greater resiliency, adaptability, and openness for change. This strategy will have a significant bearing on the course of your life.

When I made the mindset shift to opportunity vs. obstacle, it completely changed everything in my life. I always like to use the example of life happening FOR YOU and not TO YOU because when life happens TO YOU, it takes away your power, and you are left hopeless, with no way to fix or prevent it. It is as if you are under attack.

Instead, I encourage people to change their vocabulary to say life is happening "FOR ME." A real-life example of this is when I was let go from the first company I worked for as a professional. It was my first "big boy job" requiring me to show up to an office and *not* clean bathrooms.

Ha! Ha!

While unfortunate, this job loss provided me the opportunity to circle back with the company through my own consulting firm. I could have easily viewed this discharge as a negative experience, in that the company was out to get me and screw me over. Instead, I looked for the opportunity to fill a gap. I knew I was doing this company a great service as a full-time employee, but they needed to find a more economical solution. They still needed the workload to be handled, but they were trying to save money. After I was let go, I negotiated with them. I asked if I could continue to take care of the workload and bill them for a couple of hours a week through my own company, which I did not have at the time.

It was a win-win.

That way, I still made money for food, and they still had a service performed for pennies on the dollar. While I certainly did not want to be let go, it was **life setting me up for bigger success** vs. failure. I carried this mentality into my marriage and other relationships, realizing that whatever conflict I found myself facing, it was the Universe giving me a chance to improve or sharpen a certain skillset. The immediate thought that comes to mind is patience.

Many will ask God for patience to deal with their kids or spouse, but what they fail to realize is God does not provide patience. He provides the opportunity for you to develop patience.

Same thing with strength.

God does not grant you magical strength but rather provides an opportunity to develop strength. So, whenever there have been challenging times or people in my life, I know it is the Universe providing me with exactly what I need to grow. I could easily look at a tough situation and call it bad luck or coincidence, but what power would that give me and my mindset going forward? By looking at everything as an opportunity to grow, it 1.) Makes life more interesting, 2.) Provides meaning and purpose to everything I go through, which provides a sense of duty and pride.

Think about it.

You can radically alter how you take in the world around you and how you interact with it. Even the most difficult circumstances present you with opportunities to learn, develop, and prosper, if you make the effort to look for the value and potential.

Therein lies the rub.

Seek the opportunity and unlock a life that is richer and more satisfying, looming with possibility at every turn.

Throughout the course of my life, the idea is not lost on me to "make lemonade out of life's lemons." However, this simple platitude overlooks one essential component of the overarching principle of viewing life as an opportunity. And that is this: Anyone can turn a negative circumstance into a positive one, but very few ever take the time to study and scrutinize the lemons in their life. Ask yourself, "What are the lemons in my life? And why are they causing me so much grief?"

This is your pot of gold!

Understanding where the lemons are in your life and learning how to avoid them is at the heart of growth. Don't just make lemonade (willy-nilly), not without seeking to learn from the lemons. Until you grasp how they got there and how to get rid of them, you will continue to experience emotional ups and downs, which keeps you from looking for new opportunities. I mean, how much lemonade can you drink in one lifetime? It will take some time for you to successfully retrain your mind, but if you make it a habit of rethinking your life (and the lemons) every night before you go to sleep, you will find ways to push past that which holds you back.

I will use myself as an example. Five years ago, the injuries I suffered while serving in the military were the reason for my unexpected discharge. I was literally given notice of 72 hours. One day, I was serving in the U.S. Marine Corps, the next I was informed of my release.

Why?

My injuries were not improving. Upon hearing this news, I experienced a deepening depression. I was confused. I was hurt, and

I asked myself, "Why is this happening *to me*?"

I did everything required of me to ensure my duties as a Marine were successfully carried out—to the point of physical injury. And how was I repaid for my effort? I was deemed "unfit for duty" by the very organization I swore an oath to defend. It was a hard pill to swallow. The negative talk kicked in, saying, "I am worthless."

However, over the course of a couple of years, I processed my pain and the question as to why this was happening to me, and I concluded that being released from the Marine Corps was the greatest blessing in disguise.

Hindsight is 20/20.

I was being treated for a traumatic brain injury, post-traumatic stress disorder, and other physical injuries that are too painful and graphic to talk about. It was a result of the actions of several dishonorable Marines who verbally and physically assaulted me for three years. I was given a disability classification of 100 percent from the Veteran's Administration (VA). This classification has served as a comfortable padding of support for me and my family. It has allowed us to get back on our feet and get our lives back in working order.

In addition, because of the difficulty I had obtaining a disability score of 100 percent, I learned everything there is to know about the VA. I also recognized the dreadfully deficient treatment our military continue to receive daily. This knowledge and understanding made it possible for me to successfully introduce "360 Veteran," an invaluable service assisting veterans in obtaining an accurate disability rating from the VA, in a much more streamlined fashion.

Why?

Because our veterans have EARNED it. Since its inception, 360 Veteran has delivered benefits to the veteran community totalling over $1.5 billion dollars. You could say I owe my success to a handful of cowards.

I am serious!

A few jackasses in the Marine Corps acted unprofessionally and subjected me and some fellow Marines to horrible, physical abuse, particularly during training exercises. Things got out of hand, and I was taken to a hospital for a head trauma. We were removed and placed in a new location for safety concerns. Because of this hostile work environment, there were some Marines who even attempted suicide.

Talk about your toxic leadership.

Nevertheless, I have since achieved an extraordinary level of success, and I sincerely (and I do mean sincerely!) thank those cowards for "ruining" my life. Without them, I never would have been able to give back so much to the veteran community. I suppose that is why Christ instructs us to "love our enemies," embrace those who persecute us.

It is true—every word!

He just left out the part about how forgiveness and reclaiming your trauma will eventually make you incredibly wealthy and successful. I suppose that has been the most important lesson I have taken away from this. Reclaiming your trauma is something that cultures and people have done time and time again.

Repurposing trauma empowers you.

Energy is neither created nor destroyed. It can only be transformed into something else. So, if something bad happens, until that negative energy is transformed into something meaningful, you will always carry it around with you, but if you repurpose it, it can become something truly exciting! You cannot "push away" trauma or get rid of the energy created by it, but you can always transform it into something beautiful that carries you toward your purpose and passion.

I was able to do that. Repurposing my trauma allowed me to rethink my existence and alter my perception of the truth by adopting a new belief. At the time this was all taking place, I was under the impression that those involved in the abuse were terrible people, responsible for destroying my life and leaving me in a hopeless situation. But then, I shifted my perspective and took accountability. I came to believe that these people, as cruel as they were, truly blessed me. They gave me the opportunity to move from a place of pain to a place I could make a difference in the lives of thousands of people all over the world. It wouldn't have been possible under any other circumstance. I transformed negative energy into something positive.

Now that you know this, the question you need to ask yourself is, "What possibilities do I see in my life circumstances and how will I reclaim my trauma for the greater good?"

CHAPTER EIGHT
Show Me Your Books, Friends & Calendar

"Our life is the sum total of all the decisions we make every day, and those decisions are determined by our priorities."
– Miles Munroe, Bahamian evangelist

In today's world, we are in no short supply of information, ideas, and influence from around the world. It is all at our literal fingertips. The advent of the digital era has provided us with unrivaled access to resources and connections. However, it has also presented a fundamental fork in the road, which leads each of us to two critical choices, 1.) What are you consuming, and 2.) How are you spending your time?

Are you making the most of both?

I believe it is imperative that we, as individuals, are conscious of the effect our decisions have on our everyday lives and, ultimately, our lifetime achievement. That is to say, your life is shaped, in part, by the authors whose work you consume, the company you keep, and the time and effort you invest in achieving the objectives you set forth.

What Do You Choose to Consume?

Your mind is enriched and your potential for development is nurtured when you make a deliberate decision to gain knowledge, wisdom, and inspiration from books rather than the transient and frequently meaningless gratification provided by social media. This concept does not only apply to the people you surround yourself with but also to the authors and thinkers whose ideas influence your thoughts. The late American Entrepreneur, Jim Rohn, summed it up best when he said, "You are the average of the five people you spend the most time with."

The same is true of who you read and listen to.

For example, you can immerse yourself in new ideas, thoughts, and perspectives if you choose to listen to podcasts rather than just music. Podcasts provide an opportunity to learn and develop from the experiences and expertise of others, whereas music can be a wonderful source of relaxation and entertainment. That is not to say that music cannot also be a wonderful source of growth from the experiences and expertise of others.

It can be.

However, by expanding your resources to include podcasts, you expand your education and enlightenment throughout your lifetime, which broadens your horizon and perspective, making your life more fulfilling. Social media does not have the same impact or capacity. In fact, it can be an enormous time suck if you are not careful! For example, gamers may find it difficult to reconcile the idea of forgoing gameplay sessions in favor of strategy sessions. You must ask yourself, "Which will ultimately lead to greater levels of success?"

While a short break from reality (i.e., gaming) can be a good distraction from life, making time for life strategy sessions can create a game-changing break from the ordinary into the extraordinary. By forgoing gaming and participating in actual strategy sessions, whether for personal or professional development, you are putting forth an actual effort to develop real-life skills that require critical thinking and problem solving. Hence, you are prioritizing achievement over entertainment, and *that* is where you will see the big win.

Go get it!

Who Are You Spending Time With?

Considering your goals and aspirations, ask yourself, "Am I hanging around the right people? Do these people inspire and encourage me? Or do they talk me down into mediocrity?"

An effective way to know if you are engaging in a good (productive) circle of friends is to consider these three points:

1. Do they challenge you to better yourself every day?
2. Do they practice what they preach, striving to become the highest form of themselves?
3. Are they open and honest with you when others are not? In other words, are they willing to tell you the truth?

Chances are, if you answered yes to all three of these questions, you are hanging around a special bunch of people. They love and respect you too much to put up with your negative BS. They challenge you to stretch yourself to new levels, and they won't let you go it alone because they, too, are stretching outside what is comfortable.

American Entrepreneur and Motivational Speaker Tai Lopez has a theory known as the "33-percent rule." That is to say, in order to have true balance in your life, you should spend 33-percent of your time hanging around those you can mentor and guide, another 33-percent of your time should be spent hanging around peers who are at your same level and striving for more but who you can, realistically, compete with. And lastly, you should spend another 33-percent of your time hanging around your mentors, those who are on the next level of what you are striving for.

The problem many people have is in sticking around too long with the 33-percent of people they feel most comfortable with. For example, if I am hanging around my mentors all the time, men and women who are light years ahead of me and who are waking up at nine o'clock in the morning, enjoying a long breakfast, and then going golfing all afternoon, I am not dedicated to the work that will get me to where they are. The reality is they already did the work and are no longer in my shoes! If they had spent that much time hanging with their mentors when they were at my stage, they would have never gotten to where they are. And to no fault of their own, many of them have forgotten what it is like to grind seven days a week, 12 to 18 hours a day, which can hinder the real-life application of some of the advice they give. Their guidance and wisdom are invaluable because they have seen and experienced so much more than you, but if you are still in the grind, you need to open up to all three levels of expertise.

Personally, I break it down even further. I say spend time with three professional levels of people who are ahead of you. The first group of people are those who are one to five years ahead of you. They are in the grind. They are still hustling, but they are dealing with issues or have recently dealt with issues that you can glean from. The next group of people are those who are five to 10 years ahead of you. This group is nice because they are pretty well off. However, they have so much experience and practical life application to share, and this can get you thinking about the next level, all the while continuing to push your limiting beliefs about life and business. Lastly, the third group of people are 10 to 20 years ahead of you. These are the true wizards who can give advice on things that will make your journey more enjoyable, as well as prepare you for the pitfalls.

It is time to cultivate all your relationships.

Fostering relationships with people who inspire, motivate, and challenge you can have a significant effect on your overall well-being and development. I am not telling you to dump your current social circle because they do not aspire to go where you want to go and do what you want to do. I am simply telling you to invest more time in people who share your same enthusiasm for expansion, achievement, and things that make you tick. The atmosphere you cultivate for yourself is one of **the** most important factors in determining whether you will be successful in achieving your objectives. You can set the stage for a life teeming with success, fulfillment, and unrestricted potential if you invest the time to evaluate the present influences in your life, determine the areas in which you require growth, and design the ideal ecosystem for your personal life. Immerse yourself in that which fuels your soul, and the Universe will respond in your favor.

In many ways, leaving the military was difficult for me. It was one of the more challenging aspects of my transition back into civilian life. Out of necessity, military service men and women are constantly concerned about their physical well-being and level of strength. Maintaining physical fitness is ingrained in the military mindset. Therefore, many service members go to great lengths to remain fit while in service. Those who stay connected to their military community are usually in excellent physical condition. Conversely, people who completely disengage from the military community frequently have issues with their health because physical fitness is no longer within their domain of influence.

I speak from experience.

Depression and homelessness caused me to isolate. I lost the positive push from my military community, and it caused me to spiral out of control when I tried to exercise. The years following my release from the Marines left me in a physical shambles, not only because I was physically broken down, but because I gained more than 100 pounds.

I never exercised.

I was in so much pain from my injuries, any kind of physical exercise left me feeling hurt and frustrated. So, I gave up and decided to focus on the one thing I was good at, which was making money and building businesses. I spent 100 percent of my focus on working and making money for me and my family.

This is why surrounding yourself with the right people is so important to your growth as a human. Had I stayed connected to the military community and kept up my friendships, I probably would have had more motivation to stay healthy, but then again ... maybe I would have never branched out on my own and created the legacy I have.

This is me being thankful for how life happened FOR ME.

How Are You Spending Your Time?

For you to reach your objectives, it is critical that you designate blocks of time on your schedule rather than allowing life to determine when you show up or even *if* you show up. Achievement is so much easier when you can maintain your concentration and self-control in the pursuit of what is most important to you. Not only does blocking time out assist in advancing your goals, but it also instills a feeling of accomplishment and contentment in your daily life.

There are a number of factors that contribute to your level of success, including the company you keep, the literature you read, and the amount of time you devote to pursuing your ambitions. You can cultivate a setting that is conducive to development, self-improvement, and the pursuit of achievement in your life by being conscious of the decisions you make and deliberately allocating your time.

We all are given the same 168 hours in a week. So, I ask you, "What are you doing with yours, and how do you optimize your time?" Time management is what separates champions from their competitors. The way I look at it, the average bear is awake and working from 8 a.m. to 6 p.m. This means, from 5 a.m. to 8 a.m. most folks are busy doing something else (i.e., sleeping, going to the gym, getting kids ready for school), and then from 6 p.m. to 12 a.m., these same people are busy doing other things (i.e., binge watching Game of Thrones, going to the gym, sleeping, having drinks with friends). This gave me an idea of what "acceptable working hours" really are. (AKA, when I can communicate with people and complete tasks that require other humans.)

For example, from 5 a.m. to 8 a.m., I can focus on filling my mind with knowledge and resources, running errands, etc. Then, from 6 p.m. to 12 a.m., I can work on administrative tasks and projects that propel me forward. In essence, the "average bear" is only "working" eight to 10 hours a day. I, on the other hand, am literally working up to 19 hours a day.

Time management is what moved me ahead of the pack.

You cannot compete with someone who is working around the clock, never taking holidays or weekends off. This is how I was able to strategize and accomplish so much in just five years. I learned how to condense time frames.

Who said I had to be in college for four years?

If I work three times as hard, I can graduate in 1/3 the time!

Who said I only have time to focus on one full-time job?

If the job only takes up eight hours of my day, that still gives me another eight hours MINUMUM to dedicate to another job or project! Most people overestimate what they can accomplish in a week, and they underestimate what they can do in five years.

Why?

It is simply the compound effect, "the strategy of reaping huge rewards from small, seemingly insignificant actions." With this in mind, I focused my energy on working longer than anyone I knew for five years. In the first year, nothing happened. In the second year, there was no significant changes. In the third year, I started to see things happen. By the fourth year, success had been achieved. And by the fifth year, freedom was gained. My day consisted of waking up, absorbing knowledge, answering messages, working on administrative projects, beginning the "workday," answering more messages, working on business projects, going to class, doing homework, then rinsing and repeating the next day.

There was no play.

There was no "me time."

There was only WORK!

This is how I was able to condense my learning, experience, and knowledge into such a short time frame. Oftentimes, I was working with international clients throughout the night, while others were sleeping. I was getting experience and exposure to things most people had no idea about. It was Henry Wadsworth Longfellow who said, "The heights by great men reached and kept were not attained by sudden flight, but they, while their companions slept, were toiling upward in the night."

I love that!

Now that you have a comprehensive understanding of the significance of the books you read, the company you keep, and the way you maximize the 168 hours in a given week, I want to issue a challenge: Take a step back and evaluate how and with whom you spend your time. The environment you cultivate will either inspire you to flourish or cause you to fade into the background. I want to see you become your very best, and to do that, you must be more discerning and deliberate. I am here to help you do that with these three steps:

1. **Conduct an Analysis**: To start, take an honest inventory of the current relationships and influences in your life. Create a list that includes the individuals with whom you spend the most time, the books you read, the podcasts you listen to, and the forms of media you take in. Put into words the extent to which these influences either foster or inhibit growth and success.

2. **Strategize a Plan**: Next, think about your goals and what you need to succeed. Write down the kinds of relationships, influences, and surroundings that will be most beneficial to your achievement? In other words, what about a person inspires you? Make a list of the characteristics and qualities you look for in personal and professional relationships, as well as the kinds of resources and influences that will assist you in developing like attributes.

3. **Create Your Ideal Personal Ecosystem**: Once you have a good understanding of your current environment and what you need to truly succeed, you can start to map the necessary steps

in developing your ideal personal ecosystem. This may require seeking out new relationships, mentors, and/or business associates who are aligned with the goals you have set for yourself. You will likely need to alter your consumption habits, like reading more books related to your chosen field or listening to podcasts that motivate and challenge you. It won't be easy. In fact, it will take courage, consistency, and great care in sticking with your plan, but I believe in you. You can make this happen.

Ask me how I know.

When I worked in Corporate America, my standard protocol was that I punch into work at 7:55 in the morning and then punch out at 4:55 in the afternoon—no questions asked.

After all, I did clock in five minutes early! Ha! Ha!

Not one person raised an eyebrow or even questioned me.

Well, no one but me.

One day, I approached the directors and vice presidents of the organization to find out why salaried employees were clocking out after eight hours when there was still work that needed to be done. I asked the obvious question: "Why do salaried employees depart when the day is done and not when the work is done?"

Are we driven by the clock or by the work?

It was clear that the organization prioritized family time over company time (i.e., productivity) since they were almost never able to finish their tasks on time. They had cultivated a work-shy atmosphere and attitude—workload be damned. The situation was completely different at another company that I worked for. There, leadership prioritized profit, quality, efficiency, and effectiveness above all else. Nobody went home until the work was completed. You would die in the shop first.

Whatever it took to get the job done!

Once more, nobody even blinked an eye. Everybody had a smile on their face, even if was feigned for effect. Some might say this hardcore work environment is toxic, while others love it. All this to say, we are all products of our programming. You need to put yourself in a situation that supports the same ideals you do and puts forth the same work ethic toward achieving the objective. If you don't, your development will be stunted, and the garbage programming will seep into your subconscious. This could cause you to rethink everything, which could lead to feelings of resentment, uncertainty, and dread, eventually leading to different patterns of behavior on your part.

For example, if your ideal job is driven by the clock, a place you can work nine to five for $50k a year, able to drop everything at five o'clock because you have a family waiting at home, then perhaps a corporate gig is your best match. Then again, it could be that corporate life is all you know and have been conditioned to apply for.

Conversely, if you are more interested in producing extraordinary results and want to work for an organization like Tesla that recognizes employees who go above and beyond (i.e., are willing to sell their soul for $500k a year and put in exorbitant number of hours outside of the usual eight-hour window), then perhaps the corporate workplace is not for you. Again, it could be that this more stringent workplace mentality is what you have been conditioned to become.

Be careful where you lay down your roots. Ultimately, you want to thrive, working toward becoming the greatest version of yourself—whatever that looks like. And, based on your personal and professional objectives, there are certain environments that will not support and/or sustain your development. For example, when you are in a wrong job fit, it can wreak havoc on your spirit.

The term "soul crushing" comes to mind.

You know that feeling. It's like acid reflux of the soul. Let that burning sensation in your gut serve as a blaring alarm, telling you to look for your purpose elsewhere. If you are not careful of the environment you place yourself in or the people you surround yourself with or the things you consume, you will find yourself looking back and thinking, "OH SHIT! WHAT HAPPENED?"

Whether we like it or not, there are certain conundrums in life that impact our behavior and these things become automatic responses (i.e., clocking into a corporate gig, like a robot). The question I have for you is this: "Are you genuinely happy with the situation or environment that you are in right now, and is it bringing you closer to achieving your goals and dreams?"

Furthermore, I urge you to protect your ideas and ambitions. Keep them quiet if you must. Friends and family don't always get it and can often sabotage your journey. Believe me when I say, your hopes and aspirations are at risk of shrivelling up and dying if you live in an environment where you are not fully supported, which sadly is often the case. And your success is just too important not to protect it.

Besides that, it is so much better to be a living example of success versus someone who just talks about it all the time. To paint a picture, an exotic plant cannot flourish in a temperature that is not ideal for it. The same is true for people. And, unfortunately, there are many who, consciously or unconsciously, have a knack for extinguishing other people's dreams because they, themselves, are too scared to go after their own. So, surround yourself with people who get you and who have your back. You want people in your corner who will not only encourage and support you but push you to be better.

Believe me when I say, they are out there.

In conclusion, the decisions you make regarding what you put in your body and in your mind and the ways in which you spend your time have an enduring effect on the quality of your life. You can lay the groundwork for success and happiness in your life by prioritizing your personal development, acquiring more knowledge and activities focused on your goals. If you are more deliberate about the people you hang out with, the media and materials you consume, and the way in which you spend your time, you will be able to access your full potential and realize your most audacious goals.

CHAPTER NINE
Outwork, Out Strategize, Out Improve, and Outlast

"Stop comparing yourself to people with more experience than you. Every expert was once an amateur."
–Patrick Bet-David, entrepreneur

I am sorry to break it to you, ladies and gentlemen, but achievement is not for the faint of heart. It is a game that requires your full concentration, all of your energy, and unflinching dedication. The players who outwork, out strategize, out improve, and outlive their competition will emerge victorious in this game. In this chapter, we are going to discuss the significance of these four guiding principles, as well as demonstrate how their application can determine a project's failure or success.

You have to understand; individuals who achieve the most success in life did not get lucky. They merited their achievement by routinely exerting more effort than those in their immediate surroundings. It is not about being born with a silver spoon in your mouth or having natural ability. Thomas Edison alluded to it when he said, "Genius is one percent inspiration and 99 percent perspiration." That is to say, in order to make your goals a reality, you must put forth the time, effort, and sweat.

For me, it was most important that I get started right away, and once I did, I never looked back. Everyone I knew made fun of me when I announced I was giving up everything I owned in order to follow my life's ambition. People told me I was insane for attempting to accomplish so much in such a condensed timeline. My elders advised me to take things one step at a time because I was still relatively young, and I still had a lot of time ahead of me. My teachers encouraged me to postpone continuing my education until I was in a position to give my full concentration in the classroom. Most could not understand, so they carped and criticized.

Being made fun of was nothing new for me. However, being told I would never accomplish such lofty goals, lit a fire under my ass. I am perfectly good with someone mocking me or talking smack about my ideas, but when you tell me I will never achieve something I set out to do, that ticks me off. Tony A. Gaskins, Jr., motivational speaker, author, and life coach, said, "Don't expect people to understand your grind when God didn't give them your vision."

That resonated with me.

I remind myself every day that just because some have small minds and are battling limiting beliefs, does not mean I have to submit to their understanding of the world ... or of me. I say to them, "Just because YOU were not able to accomplish what you set out to do, does not mean that I can't!" In fact, I use such small-mindedness and doubt to my advantage. I wear it, like a badge of honor.

Some call it a chip on my shoulder, but they don't know me.

Whenever you set out on a mission, you must cast a vision. When you cast your vision, you will see two things: 1.) How big or small your worldview is, and 2.) Who is on the same energy level and consciousness as you are. A good rule of thumb is, if you do not feel the weight of the world on your shoulders after verbalizing your vision, you are aiming too small. My ambition was big and, certainly, FAR beyond anything I had ever set out to do.

Truth be told, I had no idea if I could make it happen.

However, I knew one thing was true. I could either die homeless on the street or chasing a dream. The latter sounded a hell of a lot better, and it wasn't until I started concentrating on the action steps rather than the outcomes that I actually began to progress. In my humble opinion and in my experience, the secret to success is in performing and producing over and over again for a long period time without expecting an instant return. We live in an age when instant gratification is king, and that is a lie in real success. The majority of people have a problem not seeing immediate results, and the reason why many people do not achieve success is because they give up too soon, allowing small impediments to derail them because they do not see sufficient outcomes in a timelier manner. They stumble upon something "better," and as a result, they alter their course of action.

Doing the work that no one else is prepared and/or willing to do is at the heart of success. For the majority of people, this means finding something you are interested in and devoting yourself to it with 100 percent diligence until you achieve your goal. For me, this meant I needed to complete every educational degree available and obtain every professional certification in the market for my particular area of expertise.

For my career, this meant starting a business from scratch

and growing it to the point where it could support me full-time. In the long run, it meant being in a position to make a difference in the lives of thousands of people by directly assisting them in achieving financial independence. And in terms of my life's purpose, it meant building a life from which I would not want to take a break. I count it as a blessing that all the goals I set out to accomplish materialized in 2017. Yes, I had to rearrange certain aspects of my life and make significant concessions along the way, but it was worth it because I was successful.

As I mentioned, I struggled with my weight. After retiring from the Marines, I gained more than 100 pounds. I had trouble sleeping. I suffered many restless nights as a result. I struggled in my romantic relationships, so I kept my inner community very small. I struggled with my mental health. I lived in constant fear that something terrible was going to happen. But at the end of the day, and after devoting myself to the hard work, I was successful in accomplishing everything I set out to do, including getting healthy again. So, as far as I am concerned, given that I am the sole creator of my narrative, that is a big win! My objectives and priorities have changed in light of the fact that I am now in a very different environment. As I move into the next stage of my life, I am emphasizing a healthy lifestyle, one that cultivates meaningful relationships. I had to ask myself the tough questions, "What am I willing to give up in order to realize my life's ambition? Or am I willing to give up on my dreams?"

Outwork

The first order of business is you need to **work harder than your competition**. This entails devoting a significant amount of time to perfecting your craft, as well as actively seeking out new information and possibilities for personal development. Challenge yourself beyond what you believe is possible and refuse to settle for mediocrity in any aspect of your life. John Wooden, legendary college basketball coach, would tell his players, "Don't measure yourself by what you have accomplished, but by what you should have accomplished with your ability."

I love that!

Consider these real-life success stories, determined individuals whose superior work ethic excelled at outworking their competitors:

Elon Musk, chief executive officer of Tesla and SpaceX, has a stellar reputation for being a hard worker. In order to maintain his high level of productivity, he frequently puts in between 80 to 100 hours of work per week and has even been known to sleep at the workplace. Musk has been able to make significant advancements in space exploration and revolutionize the industry of electric cars, thanks to his unwavering commitment to the businesses he founded.

Kobe Bryant, the late, legendary NBA player known for his tireless work ethic, began his workouts at 4 a.m. He was frequently the first person to enter the gym and the last person to leave. Bryant's unwavering commitment to honing his skills and testing the boundaries of his physical capabilities earned him the moniker "The Black Mamba." This brand of dedication helped him win five NBA championships and numerous other awards over the course of his career.

Oprah Winfrey, one of the most powerful women in the world, surmounted a challenging childhood and a number of obstacles on her path to becoming one of the most successful businesspeople in the world. Her unrelenting work ethic and unwavering commitment to her craft enabled her to construct a media dynasty that included her long-running talk show, her own television network, and her own magazine. Winfrey is revered all over the world as a result of her unwavering dedication to self-improvement and her determination to outwork everyone else.

Thomas Edison was a well-known engineer awarded more than 1,000 patents during his lifetime. He is primarily remembered for inventing the light bulb. Edison was renowned for his work ethic. He frequently worked around the clock and sometimes went stretches of days without sleep. His dedication to experimentation and his dogged pursuit of innovation resulted in the creation of ground-breaking inventions that influenced the course of history and altered the world. To demonstrate his persistence, Edison once said, "I have not failed. I've just found 10,000 ways that won't work."

Indra Nooyi, former chief executive officer of PepsiCo, is a paradigmatic illustration of a woman who outworked others to accomplish extraordinary levels of success. She was born in India, but she relocated to the United States to attend Yale University. She entered the business world in 1994 and quickly rose through the ranks before joining PepsiCo. Work ethic and strategic vision were two factors contributing to her success, which culminated in her becoming CEO in 2006. Thanks in part to Nooyi's leadership, PepsiCo substantially expanded its global presence, increased its revenue by 80 percent, and diversified its product portfolio. Both Forbes and Fortune magazine consistently placed her among the most influential women in the world.

Out Strategize

To achieve success in any endeavor, you must **have a distinct, well-thought-out strategy**. This necessitates educating yourself about your business. Become familiar with its nuances and monitor emerging trends. To remain one step ahead of your competitors, carefully consider and anticipate their next move and decisions. Sun Tzu, the great Chinese military strategist once said, "All men can see these tactics whereby I conquer, but what none can see is the strategy out of which victory is evolved." The following are some real-life individuals who have out strategized their competitors, leading them to achieve extraordinary success:

Steve Jobs, one of Apple's co-founders, was a brilliant tactician who ushered in a new era in the history of technology. Jobs' ability to anticipate market requirements and design products that captured the imagination of consumers, allowed Apple to become a dominant player in a variety of industries, including personal computers, smartphones, and digital music. Jobs also had a knack for designing products that captured the interest of consumers. His emphasis on the user experience, aesthetics, and simplicity differentiated Apple from its competitors, establishing the foundation for the company's continued success.

Jeff Bezos, founder of Amazon, continuously demonstrates an exceptional level of strategic acumen in the company's history. In the beginning, he launched Amazon as an online bookstore, but he rapidly expanded the company's product offerings. He consistently outcompeted by anticipating and capitalizing on emerging trends. Additionally, Bezos expanded Amazon's business into new areas, such as cloud processing, streaming services, and artificial intelligence research and development. Amazon has become one of the most valuable businesses in the world, thanks to Bezos' ability to foresee the long term, thus giving him the edge in making forward-thinking, strategic decisions.

Mary Barra, first female chief executive officer at General Motors (GM), is a master strategist for successfully guiding General Motors through a time of significant transition. GM made a commitment to a future with zero emissions as a direct result of her leadership, accepting the technology used in electric vehicles. Barra's concentration on innovation and her dedication to repositioning GM as a leader in the market for electric vehicles has given the company a strong competitive advantage.

Reed Hastings, co-founder and CEO of Netflix, has consistently out-strategized competitors throughout his career in the entertainment business. Under his leadership, Netflix began as a DVD rental service, before transitioning into a streaming platform and investing in original content production. He oversaw all of these major shifts. Hastings' ability to anticipate changes in the market and adapt Netflix's business strategy accordingly has allowed the company to become a dominant player in the international entertainment industry.

Sheryl Sandberg, Facebook's chief operating officer, has been an instrumental contributor to the expansion and development of the company and its overall strategy. Sandberg has played an essential role in the expansion of Facebook's userbase as well as the development of its advertising platform. Facebook has become one of the most valuable and influential businesses in the world, thanks in large part to her strategic vision and her ability to successfully execute complex initiatives.

Out Improve

The third essential component of achievement is continuous advancement. This means, you must **always be looking for new methods to improve your knowledge and expertise as well as your performance**, so you can get the most out of your life. Being humble enough to acknowledge there is always room for improvement, as well as staying hungry enough to pursue personal development in an unrelenting manner are both necessary components.

Richard Branson, British entrepreneur and business magnate, said, "You should never be satisfied with the status quo. Always push yourself to do something different and make a difference." That is to say, be open to new ideas and methods—always!

The following are real-life examples of those who have exemplified the principle of out improving, continually honing their skills and expanding their knowledge to achieve remarkable success:

Serena Williams, the great American professional tennis player, is famously known for her never-ending quest for personal growth and development. Throughout her career, Serena has constantly worked to improve her abilities by practicing her serve, groundstrokes, and fitness routines. Due in part to her commitment to improvement, Williams won 23 Grand Slam women's singles championships. She is considered one of *the* best tennis players of all time.

Warren Buffett, one of the most successful investors in the world, demonstrates a continuous dedication to self-improvement. He maintains a voracious reading habit and consumes a great deal of material on a wide range of topics, including books and articles that broaden his expertise and improve his investment strategies. Buffet's unending thirst for knowledge has undoubtedly contributed to the magnitude of his achievements in the world of finance.

Lady Gaga, singer, songwriter, and actress, has been a major contender in both the Grammys and the Oscars. Gaga demonstrates a consistent dedication to growth and improvement throughout her career. She is a front runner in her musical style, performance, and fashion. She is ever evolving. This evolution in artistry keeps her admirers interested, inspired, and intrigued. Gaga's unwavering commitment to outdoing herself and her achievements, always reinventing her persona, has helped her to solidify her position as a legend in the entertainment industry.

Satya Nadella, chief executive officer of Microsoft, is a driving force behind the company's efforts to reinvigorate and establish itself as a frontrunner in the fields of cloud computing and artificial intelligence. Nadella's dedication to never-ending improvement and innovation spurs Microsoft to expand into new industries while maintaining its position as a dominant force in the technology industry.

Misty Copeland, a pioneer in the world of ballet, made history when she became the first African-American woman to promote to the principal ballerina position at the American Ballet Theatre. Throughout her career, Copeland demonstrates a steadfast commitment to improving her technique, strength, and artistry. This has required overcoming a number of obstacles and setbacks. Her relentless pursuit of excellence has served as a source of motivation for a vast number of aspiring young dancers and has cemented her position as a pioneer in the world of ballet.

Outlast

Last but not least, we delve into durability. It is possible that this is the most essential principle of them all. The road to success is more of a marathon than a dash. It is essential that you **understand that every obstacle, setback, and failure is a part of your journey**. Embrace it and shift your mindset to a higher level of perseverance. If you keep pushing yourself, **you will finish what you started**. Legendary American Boxer, Muhammad Ali, summed it up when he said, "I hated every minute of training, but I said, 'Don't quit. Suffer now and live the rest of your life as a champion.'"

That can be you!

The following are success stories that demonstrate extraordinary resilience and perseverance in the face of adversity, thereby exemplifying the principle of outlasting the competition:

Walt Disney, the late American animator, film producer, and entrepreneur (i.e., pioneer), was plagued by a number of business failures, including bankruptcy before incorporating Walt Disney Company on October 16, 1923. Not only was his perseverance and determination key in overcoming those obstacles, but it is also the reason for so many beloved, iconic characters and stories we know and love today—the world over.

Malala Yousafzai, Pakistani activist for female education and 2014 Nobel Peace Prize laureate, was shot by the Taliban for advocating girls' education. At 17 years old, she is the youngest person to ever receive the Nobel Peace Prize and has overcome tremendous adversity to achieve this honor. Malala continues her activism, serving as an inspiration to millions of young girls (and beyond) all over the world.

Stephen King, American author of horror and supernatural fiction, had a difficult start to his career. His first book, "Carrie," was turned down for publication by 30 different publishing houses. King's perseverance and determination was fierce, and not only did he achieve unrivaled success, but his career likely outlasted many of those publishers that originally rejected his work. He has established himself as *the* standard by which horror is written. King is one of the most successful and prolific writers of all time, with over 350 million copies of his books sold worldwide.

Arianna Huffington, Greek-American author, syndicated columnist, and businesswoman, had a tumultuous professional life, including an unsuccessful run for public office and the publication of a book met with negative reviews. In spite of these obstacles, Arianna Huffington proved resilient and was able to prevail by co-founding HuffPost, an American progressive news website on May 9, 2005. Huffington later founded Thrive Global, a company centered around health and well-being after selling The Huffington Post to AOL for $315 million.

Vera Wang, former professional figure skater and world-renowned fashion designer, pursued a profession in the fashion industry and eventually became an editor at Vogue magazine. At the age of 40, Wang debuted her very own bridal fashion brand, which has since become a byword for opulence and sophistication. Her resilience in the face of adversity and her ability to adapt to emerging possibilities have helped her become one of the most powerful figures in the fashion industry.

Are you seeing a theme?

Making the decision to take another shot after an unsuccessful attempt or two or three versus giving up is what separates the successful from the unsuccessful. Every setback is but an opportunity to improve and grow—personally and professionally. It may mean taking a step back and recalibrating!

And don't forget, success requires sacrifice.

We must all make certain sacrifices in order to succeed. The important thing to remember is that you are not giving up your ambition, but rather making sacrifices for the bigger picture—the dream! Your current investment of time, energy, and resources yields a return that is many times greater in the long term.

I would like to issue another challenge: I want you to push yourself! Outwork, out strategize, out improve, and outlast your competitors. Get above the level of mediocrity and strive for excellence. Keep in mind that the only boundaries that really apply are the ones you impose on yourself. Zig Ziglar, an influential American author and public lecturer, said it best, "You don't have to be great to start, but you have to start to be great."

CHAPTER TEN
The Dichotomy of Success

"Success is going from failure to failure without a loss of enthusiasm."
—Winston Churchill, former prime minister of the U.K.

F ailure. Although the very mention of the word tends to make hearts race, we should not let that stop us from attempting to achieve what we want from life. As a general rule, we have to accept the paradox of success, which is that failing is an inevitable and essential component of the journey. We all make mistakes from time to time, but what truly characterizes us is not the stumble, itself, but how we pick ourselves up and move forward.

After all, FAIL stands for "First Attempt in Learning."

We release the energy needed for perseverance and resilience when we adopt a growth mindset and see failure as a mere steppingstone on the path to success. Consider some of the most successful individuals in the annals of humankind. In their own right, they each endured a seemingly endless stream of setbacks, but emerged from each one wiser and better equipped to deal with future challenges. Again, Thomas Edison, who is credited for having invented the light bulb, said, "I have not failed. I have just found 10,000 ways that won't work."

Edison was aware that failure was an essential component of

the process, and he embraced it in order to develop something we all use, if not take for granted to this day. Some of you are able to read this book right now because of Edison's persistence over trial and error.

Winston Churchill, another powerful example of how failure is what we make it, once said, "Success consists of going from failure to failure without loss of enthusiasm." This is a compelling quote that exemplifies the idea that failure is something you own. If you go into the situation with the mindset that you are doomed to fail and that nothing will improve and there is nothing you can do about it, then you can expect to get just that—nothing. If, on the other hand, however, you look at each setback as an opportunity to learn something new and keep working toward your goal, you will ultimately achieve success. You must welcome failure with open arms and apply it to your life.

If you haven't read Jocko Willinks' "Extreme Ownership," I suggest you get a copy of it today. I am serious. Put down my book and order a copy right now. When we assume ownership of our mistakes, we accept responsibility for the results as well as the knowledge gained from them. We don't shirk responsibility for our errors because we are cowards, but rather, we view them as opportunities for personal development. Nelson Mandela, former president of South America and anti-apartheid activist, said, "Do not judge me by my successes; rather, judge me by the number of times I've fallen down and gotten back up again."

To achieve real success, the kind that transforms your life, you have to be prepared to challenge yourself beyond your comfort zones and face your deepest, most irrational fears and anxieties. If failure is a necessary component of the path that leads to achievement, you must courageously act in accordance because you have an obligation to acknowledge its value to the world at large. Keeping in mind that success is a paradox, and welcoming failure is a necessary step toward personal development, the process will ask much of you. However, if you maintain your commitment to the goal, reflect on and improve upon your past actions and forge ahead, you will begin to see progress. Embrace the discipline of learning from your mistakes, and you will discover the freedom to be successful.

Discipline equals freedom.

One unfortunate misconception modern society has ingrained in our brains is that failure is a bad thing, something that should be avoided at all costs. This mistaken belief has been pushed on us for a variety of reasons. From our childhood to our educational system to our workplace, we have been told that failing is not an option, and it has had a negative impact on how we respond to challenges and how we recover as a result. For instance, in our educational system, the emphasis on standardized testing and assigning grades to work assignment causes us to believe that the most important aspect of learning is in earning the highest possible score. This mindset can paralyze a student's ability to take risks and learn from their mistakes. It can cause a student unnecessary anxiety because they are afraid of getting a poor score or failing a test.

In a similar vein, we are frequently made to believe that

promotions and success in the workplace are reserved exclusively for those individuals who never fail. This has the potential to stifle innovation and creativity, producing a climate of risk-averse employees. When folks are scared of failing, they are hesitant to try new things, share new ideas, or think outside the box.

Failure is associated with negative professional outcomes.

I hope to change that way of thinking because we only learn, develop, and become more resilient as a result of our past mistakes and setbacks. Accepting our own personal shortcomings and growing from them is an essential element of making forward progress. I have said this before, and I will say it again because it bears repeating: "In the end, the goal is not to be perfect. The goal is to be better today."

So, I ask you, "Are you making a conscious effort to revise your conception of failure?" It takes courage to combat the detrimental indoctrination to which we have all been subjected. It is of the utmost importance that you cultivate and prioritize learning and development over perfection, not only in your personal life but also in the business you conduct. If you take steps in this direction, you will cultivate an atmosphere in which failure is not regarded as a setback but rather as an opportunity for development and improvement.

Embrace an infinite mindset.

This mindset emphasizes the bigger picture and is characterized by an awareness of the fact that there is no "destination" in life. Instead, it is a never-ending process of growing, becoming more knowledgeable, adaptable, and mature. When we adopt this mentality, we are more likely to accept failure as a normal and inevitable part of the process, rather than a definitive verdict on our capabilities as individuals.

We can experience failure without being labeled a failure.

Personally, I see my entire existence as being nothing but success, even the hard parts. I was one of the youngest martial arts instructors at the age of nine. At the age of 16, I became the youngest assistant manager at a major food retailer. I graduated high school early at the top 20 of my class and with honors. I graduated at the top of my military class and was meritoriously promoted. I overcame suicidal thoughts and homelessness. I became a world champion in martial arts, and I ranked nationally in discus in both junior high and high school. I can honestly say that my life has been filled with many wonderful "opportunities" and "experiences" that others might see as setbacks, and these are just some of the significant milestones I have reached along the way. It wasn't easy, even though to some it may have appeared that way.

Most people I know are unaware of the countless hours I spent after school performing and engaging in rigorous physical training required of world champions. They had no idea that, at nine years old, I was experiencing a mental breakdown and struggling with impostor syndrome while instructing an adult martial arts class, people who paid for instruction by a world champion. For years, no one watched as I practiced javelin, shot put, discus, and other throwing events five nights a week. They do not know I worked two jobs (around the clock) in high school, covering every shift I could during breaks and vacations. They had no idea of the sleepless nights I spent studying for tests, attempting to overcome crippling anxiety and panic attacks. They did not see me in the quarters after school because I was in my room learning the Marine Corps Orders (MCOs) and the Uniform Code of Military Justice (UCMJ). They were not there when I burst into tears in the middle of the night because I was unable to exercise control over my thoughts, nor were they aware of the terrible acts those thoughts were leading me to.

Most people did not see me sleeping in the backseat of my car in parking lots, hoping that no one would contact the police and praying that my wife and I would be able to keep warm through the night. Most will never know or appreciate the 10 years I opted *not* to have a social life or take vacations. How could they know I exchanged the enjoyment of hobbies for my ambition to succeed? They never knew I spent all of my earnings on furthering my education. They were not with me in the gap, the months in which my wife and I had no customers or employees to support our businesses. How could anyone know we, 360 Veteran, would be publicly accused of "scamming" our nation's military veterans and our accusers would attempt to shut us down, resulting in a lack of financial resources for our organization.

Even as you read this now, I wonder if you have any idea how many sleepless nights it took me to write my story or expose the anguish felt in sharing this journey with you. I have never disclosed the traumatic experiences I endured as a child. I have never discussed the suicidal ideations I had, and I have definitely never given anyone an inside look into my mind and the things I have struggled with.

The Dichotomy of Success

Why, then, am I sharing them with you now?

It is my hope that something in this work will strike a chord with you in one way, shape, or form. I have faith my experience will motivate you to take control of your life, rethink the circumstances you find yourself in, and get you started on a path toward transforming your reality. We have all been dealt cards that none of us asked for, and our lives are generally pretty miserable as a result. There are some that are undeniably worse than others. The wonderful thing about life and our thoughts is that they are always open to new experiences and new ways of thinking.

In light of my early existence (i.e., my background, family, financial status, and a handful of other factors), I should likely be working some sort of menial job, earning just enough money to keep myself afloat, like so many people. The plan would have been to take a two-week vacation every year, put money into my 401(k), celebrate the holidays with family, and then do it all over again until I reached the age of 67 years old, at which point I would eventually retire. My actual existence, in spite of all those factors, is another story!

Why?

Because I made the deliberate decision to work hard toward accomplishing my objectives and achieving my goals. I gave up a lot in order to get to where I am today, and you can do the same. Now, you might be thinking, "I have already given up a lot!"

Well, that's great!

Think about where you were before you made the commitment, and then consider where you could be if you continue to put forth a massive effort. Life is a battleground. Every single day, you have to decide whether you want to fight for something extraordinary or throw your hands up in the air and run away. It is time for you to stand tall, look deep within yourself, and bring forth the magnificence that resides within you.

You need to want it more than anything else, my friend.

Eric Thomas, motivational speaker, author, and minister, said it best, "When you want to succeed as bad as you want to breathe, then you will be successful." You have to be prepared to make sacrifices and persevere through the pain. Tackle your anxieties and difficulties head on!

Do not settle for mediocrity!

Mediocrity is a disease that will keep you chained to a life of unfulfilled potential. Get rid of those restraints! Own up to the extraordinary potential that was embedded in you at the moment of your conception. You might be experiencing some discomfort right now, but you should know that this discomfort has the potential to turn into strength, and that strength will transport you to heights that you did not believe were possible. You are closer to your breakthrough than you realize.

Stay strong, and don't give up!

You are designed for greatness! Never stop striving to achieve it, and never give in to the temptation to settle for anything less. The world is looking forward to seeing your brilliance, and now is the time to demonstrate who you are and what you are capable of. However, don't wait for others to help you get there.

You will have to go this road alone.

Make a commitment to yourself today—no more excuses, no matter the uncertainty of the situation. No more worry. It is time for you to rise above circumstance and take ownership of the triumph that is waiting for you. Do not forget, dear friend, glory is eternal, but sacrifice is only temporary. The most important thing to remember is that YOU have the ability to alter your circumstance, thereby constructing the life you have always dreamed of having. Although, it is not a pleasant or simple path to take, it is worth it. You have the ability to shift your mentality, the way in which you perceive the world around you, and this power supersedes all others.

It also makes the journey so much more enjoyable.

Going forward, you are in control of the situation. Now, let me ask you this: "What are you going to do to improve your life today?"

EPILOGUE
The Next Journey

*"When you say 'yes' to others, make sure you
are not saying 'no' to yourself."*
–Paulo Coehlo, Brazilian lyricist & novelist

Congratulations on taking the first significant step in getting rid of your BS! While my book has walked you through the weeds of positive change, inspiring personal and professional grown, I am not going to just abandon you after having given you a road map to independence from belief systems that no longer suit you. In addition, I will not solicit your company or invite you to attend my "super, awesome five-day workshop for only $995!" I am, however, going to put you to the test by requesting that you carry out the exercises listed below. These activities will help drive you forward, reframing your life and redefining your truth, just as it did for me.

It is possible that some of these workouts will feel strange. If they do, that is a good sign. It means you are challenging yourself to participate in activities that are outside your comfort zone. I find it helpful to remind you that the sooner you teach yourself to be okay with being uncomfortable, the simpler life becomes. I am confident that by the time you finish these activities, you will have a fresh perspective of your life. You will experience a sense of gratitude as well as insight, and who knows, maybe even a breakthrough will occur for you! The best part is that I won't charge you for using these tools and resources, and I won't ask for anything in return. Alright, maybe I will ask for a five-star book review, but other than that, I am not going to ask for anything. (Ha!) This reminds me of something Gary Vaynerchuk, American serial entrepreneur and five-time, best-selling author, said in an interview: "When you give, you give. When you're asking, you're asking. Don't be half pregnant in your giving. And don't be half pregnant in your asking when you want to sell something."

Honestly, this book is a sincere attempt at providing you value, the same value I discovered when completing these exercises and the same value I provide all my customers.

So, let's get started!

Exercise #1: Map Your Story (3 hours)

The first exercise is to make a map of your story. On a sheet of construction paper or poster board, draw your life story, beginning at birth to present day. Use your imagination and focus on the most significant moments in time. When you do this for the first time, do not include a lot of detail. Instead, focus on your life year by year (i.e., Year One: I learned to walk. Year Four: I played my first team sport. Year Six: I broke my arm and stayed overnight in the hospital.) You will likely experience flashbacks to significant events while you move through this process. I strongly advise you keep a record of all the events, even the traumatic and tragic ones. The more story points you have, the more enjoyable and gratifying the next phase of the activity will be for you.

In addition, I recommend setting a timer for 90 minutes. Try not to spend too much time ruminating on the past. Simply write down significant events, mapping it out onto the sheet of paper. Visualize yourself going back through the years and experiencing each of these moments all over again. Take note of how your facial muscles relax when you smile and how your body tenses up in other areas of your life. Feel the waves of happiness, sadness, anxiety, and exhilaration wash over your entire body. Write down any significant life experiences that leave you with a profound sense of emotion and make a note of them as they occur. After you have completed this step, take some time to gather your thoughts and find your center before moving onto the next phase of this exercise.

Now, turn the sheet of paper over. On the backside, go through that same story map, but instead of simply describing each event, write down in more detail what you learned from the experience. For example: When I was 13 years old, I got caught cheating on my final exam, and as a result, I got kicked out of school. The lesson: I learned that taking shortcuts in life is almost never acceptable.

Write down the lessons (i.e., bullet points) you learned in each life event on a separate sheet of paper. Now, go through each bullet point, asking yourself these simple questions: 1.) Does this "life lesson" benefit or hurt me today? 2.) Is the conviction (i.e., BS) I "interpreted" from this occurrence the correct one? 3.) Could there be another way to interpret the results of this experiment?

At the end of three hours, you will have 30 minutes to look back on your life and relive it using this map. Spend some time thinking about each of the line items you wrote down. Once you are finished, return to your storyboard and rewrite a new line of BS based on what you have learned. After considering your assumptions about the event in question, rewrite what you believe should be the most important lesson learned. After you finish this step, read through your narrative one more time, keeping in mind the fresh interpretations you have developed. So, instead of saying, "When I was six years old, I broke my arm playing soccer. I learned I should not have been so careless," try saying "When I was six years old, I broke my arm playing soccer. I should have been more careful by honing my skills to outperform my rivals."

Whatever it is you believe is the correct response, and however you decide to visualize the events that have occurred in your life, *that* is your new narrative. This new narrative better supports your objectives and ambitions, welcoming a new truth that empowers your life. The best part is that you can keep doing this over and over again as you move forward, checking to see if the interpretations and assumptions you are making are helping or hurting you in the present day. If you find they are not helping you, you can always rewrite your storyline because **you are the author**. Years from now, when you look back on this activity, remember to take what you have learned and use it in your everyday life. This road mapping of your story and your life lessons has limitless room for the things that happen FOR

YOU, and you always have the option to reframe how you look at life in a more positive light.

Get out there and make some changes to your life!

Exercise #2: Mindfulness

STOP! Stop whatever you are doing that is causing you anxiety and notice what is going through your mind! Pay attention to your breathing. I am willing to bet your breath is quick and shallow.

How do I know?

The majority of people rarely use their entire lung capacity to breathe, which results in a variety of problems. The most significant of which is fatigue. Think about it; if your brain and the rest of your body require oxygen to function properly, and if you are only supplying your body with half of its oxygen needs, it can only function for so long.

Why else do you think we yawn?

We yawn to supply our bodies with the necessary amount of oxygen to function. We require an injection of blood and an infusion of oxygen. What exactly is the connection of breath and practicing mindfulness? Allow me to demonstrate.

Over the course of this next week, monitor your breathing by setting an alarm on your watch, phone, and/or another electronic device. When the alarm goes off, stop what you are doing and notice your breathing. Be honest with yourself.

If you aren't honest, this experiment won't work.

When you monitored your breathing, were you actually breathing deeply, or were you taking short, quick breaths of air? Develop a deep awareness of your breath. Concentrate on breathing more deeply, until your mind gets clearer, and your negative thoughts start to slip away. This is just one easy way to practice meditation. Some have the misconception that practicing meditation calls for an in-depth knowledge of mystical arts as well as a significant amount of quiet patience. However, the most accomplished meditators are "always" in a state of meditation because they are constantly conscious of their existence, feelings, thoughts, and actions.

This is mindfulness at its best!

When you pay attention to your breathing, you bring light to your surroundings, your thoughts, your actions, the sensation of the wind hitting your face, the energy of the people around you, and other similar factors. The vast majority of people go through life oblivious to the surrounding energies and sensations because they spend their lives living inward, consumed by their own BS. When you make an effort to appreciate each breath, you open up a whole new level of gratitude for the most basic of human needs, including your next breath. Stopping what you are doing and forcing yourself to become aware of life around you may seem a little strange at first, but as is the case with most new habits, if you do this consistently over the next month, it will become more natural, not to mention beneficial as you pause and enjoy your life on a more instinctual level.

I promise you.

I am not preaching life according to Pollyanna. I am the first to tell you that life has its ups and downs. However, in order to get the most out of your life, you need to appreciate the range of emotions and sensations that come along with both the highs and lows. The meaning you give to your feelings is what ultimately determines your level of happiness. The wonderful part is that you have complete control over what that meaning is, putting you in an enlightened state of mind.

Now, get out there, and start taking charge of your own life.

Exercise #3: List the Three Best Things

Go out and get a pad of sticky notes to carry around with you wherever you go. As you go about your daily routine, make a note of the top three best things that happen FOR YOU throughout the day. Start as soon as possible. As soon as you wake up and roll out of bed, start writing!

You might be thinking, "Steven, it is only six in the morning, and I have barely gotten out of bed. There is nothing for me to write!"

To which I would reply, "Dive deeper; really think about it."

Did you wake up? Yes?

Good.

Did you wake up without the usual migraine? Yes?

Good.

Did you wake up on time? Yes?

Good.

Do you see where I am going with this? There are three

positives that will get you moving in the right direction. Use your imagination, but make sure you are pushing yourself. Ask yourself; did you find food in the refrigerator when you woke up? Did you wake up with a roof over your head? Did you wake up in a warzone? Did you wake up to flooding in your basement? Did a fire destroy your home the night before? Did you wake up with excruciating back pain? EVERY SINGLE DAY, there are a variety of occurrences that take place in our lives—good and bad. Consider how wonderful life was **FOR YOU** today, and how privileged you are when you can clearly see how other people's lives are falling apart around you. As the day progresses, remain focused on the things that take place **FOR YOU**.

Have you started the day with your go-to breakfast?

Good!

On the drive to work, did you narrowly escape rush hour?

Good!

Continue to make a list of the positive experiences that transpire FOR YOU, and at the end of each day, just before you go to sleep, choose the three that stand out above the rest.

Pull off the sticky notes and write them down in a journal to be kept next to your bed. That way, when you wake up tomorrow morning (and every morning after), you will already have a reminder of the good the day has in store.

This activity might sound completely insane, but by doing it, you are training your brain to find extraordinary things even in the most mundane aspects of everyday life. There are so many miracles that take place around us every day, yet our worldview is so limited that we fail to recognize them. This practice is designed to improve your energy level, make you more appreciative, and retrain your mind to focus on the positive.

Again, if you give this 30 days, you will start to see life from a completely different perspective. You have just entered a world filled with greatness and opportunities.

Go out into the world and change your truth.

Bonus Exercise: You Matter

The following physical activity, once incorporated into your normal routine, can actually be rather enjoyable. I strongly recommend you do this first thing in the morning, so to get your day off to a stress-free and useful start. Don't worry; I will never advise you to wake up at 2:30 a.m. like Mark Walberg.

Ha! Ha!

I call this exercise the "4 x 15." If you complete it correctly, you will have accomplished more in the first hour of your day than what the vast majority of people complete in 24 hours. Not only will it provide you a daily boost, but more importantly, it will retrain your way of thinking. This does demand a significant amount of self-control, but if you stick with it, I guarantee you will be rewarded with a revitalized sense of self-worth and confidence.

Here we go!

Roll out of bed and move around. Do something active—jump, run, do pushups, take a walk, punch a bag or dance in the living room for a total of 15 minutes. Next, stretch, practice mindfulness, engage in self-reflection and self-affirmation, meditate, or some other similar activity for another 15 minutes. Then, read, write, keep a journal, pray, write down your daily to dos, design your whiteboard, or paint for the next 15 minutes. Finally, find a video or a piece of music that motivates you. Do something that will make you laugh and smile.

These simple actions are all pretty straightforward, and I am willing to bet that by engaging in these four 15-minute blocks, your day-to-day life will appear less challenging. By prioritizing one or two of these activities, those things you enjoy the most, you will bring yourself back to center before the day even begins. And you won't have to beat yourself up for not finding time in the day to do what you love. As a matter of fact, by accomplishing them first thing in the morning, you will feel invigorated, inspired, open, and nourished. Think of it this way; you are filling up your proverbial petrol tank and performing the necessary maintenance that keeps your vehicle running smoothly. The same is true of your physical body; if you do not provide yourself the fuel you need, your body will not function properly. It will start to deteriorate and make strange sounds if the parts are not lubricated and maintained. Your mind, body, and spirit are all affected in the same way.

So, make sure you take care of you.

Too often people experience mental breakdowns after huge

success because they did not take care of themselves along the way. Give this new addition to your schedule 30 days to settle in and observe how it works with the rest of your life. Because it covers every aspect of self-care in just one hour, it is incredibly feasible for the vast majority of people to carry out.

Give it a shot!

Pay attention to how it makes you feel, especially in light of the fact that you will be doing something every day to improve yourself without having to sacrifice too much. You have entered the world of realistic self-care.

You're welcome!

Now, seriously, get out there and give your mind, body, and soul the fuel each needs to flush out the BS!

www.ingramcontent.com/pod-product-compliance
Lightning Source LLC
Chambersburg PA
CBHW060815050426
42449CB00008B/1669